Working with Destiny

The Golden Blade 1997

Anthroposophy springs from the work and teaching of Rudolf Steiner. He describes it as a 'path of knowledge, to guide the spiritual in the human being to the spiritual in the universe.'

The aim of this yearly journal is to bring the outlook of anthroposophy to bear on questions and activities of evident relevance to the present, in a way which may have a lasting value. It was founded in 1949 by Charles Davy and Arnold Freeman, who were its first editors.

The title derives from an old Persian legend, according to which King Jamshid received from his god, Ahura Mazda, a golden blade with which to fulfil his mission on earth. It carried the heavenly forces of light into the darkness of earthly substance, thus allowing its transformation. The legend points to the possibility that humanity, through wise and compassionate work with the earth, can one day regain on a new level what was lost when the Age of Gold was supplanted by those of Silver, Bronze and Iron. Technology could serve this aim; instead of endangering our planet's life, it could help to make the earth a new sun.

Working with Destiny

The practice of karma research

The Golden Blade No. 49

Edited by William Forward
and Andrew Wolpert

Floris Books

First published in 1996 by Floris Books.

© 1996 Floris Books, Edinburgh
All rights reserved. No part of this publication may
be reproduced without the prior permission of
Floris Books, 15 Harrison Gardens, Edinburgh.

British Library CIP Data available

ISBN 0-86315-241-1
ISSN 0967-6708

Printed in Great Britain
by Cromwell Press, Melksham, Wilts.

Contents

Editorial notes   7

The karmic core of anthroposophy
Virginia Sease   13

Karma research
Nick Thomas   32

Intimations in images
Nothart M. Rohlfs   37

Trauma versus karma
Hans Peter van Manen   46

Angels amongst us
Hartwig Schiller   57

Karma and the Internet
Dorit Winter   77

Shakespeare and world destiny
Richard Ramsbotham   102

Karma and the mystery dramas
John Gee   121

Notes on the contributors   127

Editorial notes

To represent the knowledge of reincarnation and karma for the twentieth century and into the future was the essence of Rudolf Steiner's task. Lecturing and writing not only for those who had already committed themselves to a path of inner development, this Christian initiate also addressed the public on themes that had till then been the preserve of secret brotherhoods. He knew that the interest in esotericism and the growing capacity to be individually responsible in matters of occult science demanded that he speak about how the faculties of supersensible cognition could be attained, as well as about the results of his clairvoyant research.

In books such as *Knowledge of Higher Worlds* and *Occult Science* as well as in lectures and numerous other publications, Rudolf Steiner describes very specific exercises to develop the powers of thinking and observation, to penetrate the soul forces with greater consciousness and to meditate with full presence of mind. It is characteristic of spiritual science, just as with natural science, that every stage of investigation is consciously observed and understood so that the processes, as well as the result, are known. This is what distinguishes spiritual science from mysticism and other excursions into the occult, in which only the destination is experienced and the journey is veiled. The salient characteristic of all these exercises is that they are to be practised regularly and repeatedly, and that they do not produce instant clairvoyance. Even the very specific karmic exercises that Rudolf Steiner also gave will not lead to sudden revelations of previous incarnations. It is much more the case that the consciously willed faithfulness to such freely undertaken inner discipline may lead to a certain soul sensitivity and spirit receptivity that help to make sense, to discern meaning and be awake to intimations of the workings of destiny.

This issue of *The Golden Blade* is dedicated to the exploration of destiny and karma manifestations that have revealed themselves to the practice of such spiritual–scientific research methods. We offer no sensational secrets about past lives, firstly, because mere curiosity without responsibility is inimical to the faculties of clairvoyance and, secondly, because, when such knowledge has been won, it is treated with the discretion that protects it from scandal-mongering. One is even tempted to say that sensational revelations are *prima facie* suspect because the capacity to win karmic insight is inseparably linked with the knowledge of how to handle such information appropriately. The reassuring aspect of this is that any occultist who invites and expects attention on the basis of claiming who he was in a previous life is certainly a charlatan, either lying or misusing the truth. No initiate who serves human evolution will allow the glory of a past incarnation to lend credibility to his present endeavours. While the achievements of previous lives form the possibilities and tasks for succeeding incarnations, the accomplishments of each life must speak for themselves.

It is the epistemology of letting the matter speak for itself that eschews a guru whose superior consciousness displaces mine; that disdains the ouija board which purports to tell me 'who' and 'what' but not 'how'; and that mistrusts the claims of spontaneous or hypnotically induced revelations of previous lives, precisely because in all these the process of arriving at the information is not part of what is seen. If the karmic intimation does not validate itself, then there is a dependence on an unknown intermediary. That is not science: the matter does not speak for itself. It is a characteristic of karmic research that the organs of spiritual perception have reached a degree of sensitivity that the observation is self-evidently reliable, axiomatic. The analogy with natural science is pertinent and exact: if the process of observation is not axiomatically valid there can be no scientific process or hypothesis to be proved or refuted.

It is an uncomfortable but unavoidable fact that, in this area of growing public awareness, intense interest and speculation, there are unhealthy spiritual forces in the wings, ready to take advantage of ingenuous and untrained prospectors. Their credulity, although well intended, becomes fertile ground for the counter-evolutionary forces to plant partially true stories. The apparently most compelling external circumstantial evidence that corroborates the revelation of a previous earth life (there turned out really to be a secret passage under the cellar!) only proves that the story corresponds to certain facts. It does not prove that the individual to whom it is revealed had the supposed karmic connection with it. To be blunt: one can be unwittingly possessed. In this way the timely knowledge of reincarnation is undermined and wrecked by pseudo-experiences. The strategy is that when these spurious revelations are eventually exposed, they will, in the process, discredit the whole notion of repeated earth lives. It serves no good purpose to play down these attempts to cut us off from our true spiritual heritage: knowledge of reincarnation and karma is the foundation of our future culture.

Hans Peter van Manen, whose article on regression therapy explores this theme, is well known for his own investigations of the workings of destiny. In addition to his much acclaimed book *Twin Roads to the Millennium* (Rudolf Steiner Press, 1988) he has also published a lecture given in 1991 under the title *Marie Steiner: Her Place in World Karma* (Temple Lodge Press, 1995). This is an exemplary piece of karma research, in which he describes the careful processes of observation and modestly but clearly expressed hypothesis in such a way that the journey and the destination are experienced as integral. The content of that lecture provides the complementary historical perspective on the article by Virginia Sease, which illustrates most illuminatingly how the laws of karma, in a particular situation, can be seen to run their course through lives of individuals, facilitating their destinies. The theme of principles at work in karma is taken up by Nick Thomas, who explores the individual manifestations of such forces which are non-mechanical, non-deterministic, unpredictable, and yet disclose their lawfulness.

The paradox of inevitability and unpredictability is one of the features of karma that Hartwig Schiller identifies in his contribution based on his experience as a teacher. The keenly observed aspects of collegial life at the level of individuals, place and time hold good at a more general level for any group of individuals who assemble to work together. However, a College of Teachers in a Waldorf school is one of those few collegial communities where the ideas of reincarnation and karma can be taken for granted and are actively worked with socially and pedagogically. A certain constellation of colleagues in a particular school at a specific time is a manifestation of karmic forces from the past, ready at every moment to serve the future destinies of the institution, the teachers and the pupils.

At any moment one can have an intuitive grasp of one's freedom to accept, unite oneself with, and serve one's destiny. The idea that we took certain resolves before coming to earth, that we have prebirth intentions which we do not immediately remember, is the secret that solves the paradox of freedom and destiny. Freedom at this level means to be unimpeded and awake to recognize the direction we have chosen. Accepting the idea that we have participated in the shaping of our lives is already a first stirring into that wakefulness. The very notion that there may be a purpose to the hard knocks of life and that we, ourselves, may have purposed them is part of the freedom that is compatible with destiny.

Not of least significance in our self-directed role are the encounters we have with other individuals. Also within the wider pedagogical context, Dorit Winter explores what the consequences to the quality and potential of our meetings might be if they are substituted by virtually real intercourse on the Internet. Her clear and dispassionate analysis of the threat to the sanctity of the human encounter is imbued with love for the truth that will not shirk the challenge to engage with the opposition. Just what is at stake is the theme of Nothart Rohlfs' article, in which he describes the images and impressions that disclose themselves if we work consciously with the potential in our meetings with others. Awakening to the reality of another person through the schooled sensitivity Rohlfs has practised is something of an antidote to the dangers of the virtual interactions that Winter exposes. It is a Michaelic deed to undertake that schooling of sensitivity not instead of but alongside the unavoidable electronic encounters.

If the world is a stage for the drama of our destiny, then a play inspired by karmic themes makes the theatre a highly potentized microcosm. To compare and contrast the plays of Shakespeare and Rudolf Steiner's mystery dramas would surely be a rewarding enterprise. In the articles by John Gee and Richard Ramsbotham two very different approaches to destiny are explored through drama. In the one an actor describes the experiences of representing the destiny events of reincarnating individuals. In the other a scholar discerns the manifestations of macrocosmic events through the characters in some of the plays.

The timeliness of our theme for this issue was borne out by the encouragement we received from our speaking partners and by the enthusiasm of our contributors. The momentum is not exhausted by this issue. We have decided to devote next year's *Golden Blade,* the fiftieth edition, to a continuation of the theme, with further contributions arising out of practical karma research, and hope to include, among others, articles by doctors, therapists and priests, whose work is based on the active consideration of karmic influences.

This is the last issue to be published with our colleagues at Floris. We wish to thank them most warmly for their support and unstinting editorial advice and assistance. The new publishing arrangements have not been finalized at the time of going to press but we expect the 1998 issue to be available through the usual channels towards the end of 1997.

W.F., A.W.

The karmic core of anthroposophy

Rudolf Steiner and Marie Steiner 1900–1907

Virginia Sease

Especially in the last decade there has been a growing awareness that Rudolf Steiner's task required the accompanying strength of Marie von Sivers-Steiner's contribution in order to sink roots into the spiritual–cultural soil of the twentieth century. In regarding certain central aspects of this mutual work we can perceive how basic laws of karma are in action. Part of the following considerations were included in lectures given for the Anthroposophical Society in Switzerland and for the Section for the Arts of Eurythmy, Speech and Music in winter and spring 1996 at the Goetheanum. They assume that the reader is aware of Marie von Sivers' (as of 1914 Marie Steiner) speech and drama studies and work in Paris.[1]

A destiny encounter for Marie von Sivers

An early characteristic of Marie von Sivers in her own words was:

> Before I left Petersburg I tore up my diary from that time which contained questions about the meaning of life and

kept only the last page, on which was written: *Où trouver la vérité?* [Where to find the truth?][2]

Her search led her in the late 1890s to discover *The Great Initiates* by the French writer and mystic, Edouard Schuré (1841–1929), which he published in 1889. Even now, a century later, this magnificent work continues to form a bridge for many seekers of spiritual truth. Here a literary link is made to the ancient mystery places whose teachers acted as guides for humanity. Marie von Sivers, whose linguistic prowess encompassed verbal and written excellence in Russian, French, German, English and Italian, found not only the content of Schuré's work deeply inspiring but also his poetic language.[3] This impression was enhanced when, while vacationing in the summer of 1900 on the Latvian coast of the Baltic Sea, she read Schuré's most recent work, *Théâtre de l'âme,* which contained two dramas, *'Les enfants de Luzifer'* (The Children of Lucifer) and *'La soeur gardienne'* (The Guardian of the Threshold). She was so moved by *'Les enfants de Luzifer'* that she wrote to Schuré to ask for permission to translate it into German. Thus ensued a correspondence between Edouard Schuré, at that time fifty-nine years old and very well known, and the unknown Marie von Sivers, exactly thirty-three years old.

In an early letter from mid-October 1900, Edouard Schuré writes in response to a letter from Marie von Sivers:

> The impetus of your thoughts and the finesse of your feeling indicate that you belong to those special souls, who seek the meaning of life beyond banality and those regions which are forced upon us by the necessity of fate, in order to rise up to an ideal which you have freely chosen and which you try with determination to realize.[4]

Then some weeks later in November 1900:

> When a translator is filled with such noble enthusiasm for the ideas of a text which he is translating, then he is more

than a translator, he becomes an interpreter and co-worker of the author.[5]

The path to Rudolf Steiner

Soon thereafter Marie von Sivers asked Edouard Schuré for his opinion concerning contemporary spiritual societies and if one could profit from membership in any one of them. The response was that he himself belonged to the Theosophical Society. Therefore, in the late autumn of 1900, when Marie von Sivers was in Berlin and found an announcement in a newspaper concerning the Theosophical Society, she contacted the leaders of the Berlin Branch, Count and Countess Brockdorff, and discovered that Rudolf Steiner, then 39 years old, would be holding lectures. It is interesting to picture this gracious, attractive, highly gifted young lady from the upper circles of society joining the small group of dedicated Theosophists in the Brockdorff's large Berlin apartment. It was probably somewhat sensational! Her recognition of Rudolf Steiner's spiritual stature was instantaneous.

Even as Marie von Sivers' translations into German of Edouard Schuré's dramas meant a turning point for his international recognition, so too for Rudolf Steiner did she bring about the next and most vital step into the future. He speaks about this moment years later in a lecture (11 October 1915)[6] when he alludes to a conversation with Marie von Sivers in the autumn of 1901 at the home of a theosophist. Marie von Sivers always spoke of this destiny conversation as the 'Chrysanthemum Tea' conversation, as so many chrysanthemums decorated the room! The tea itself was to commemorate the founding of the Theosophical Society on 17 November 1875. Marie von Sivers asked if it were not necessary to call into life a spiritual movement expressly for Europe, as Theosophy was so connected with eastern spirituality. Rudolf Steiner responded that he could only be for such a movement that would connect decidedly with western Christian occultism and which he would develop further. Through this question Rudolf Steiner knew that the person had appeared who could carry his own spiritual task with him. This was in a sense a prerequisite for the task itself. He referred to Marie von Sivers from the beginning as co-founder in the work. Johanna Mücke, a trusted co-worker from the early days in Berlin, recalled a statement by Rudolf Steiner:

> Therewith [that is, Marie von Sivers' question] I received the possibility to work in the way which I imagined. The question was presented to me and I could, true to spiritual laws, begin to give the answer to such a question.[7]

The journey from this moment on, beginning with the request in 1902 at the Theosophical Congress in London that Rudolf Steiner assume the office of General Secretary of the Theosophical Society in Germany, Austria and Switzerland, is well documented in *The Story of my Life* and in Guenther Wachsmuth's biography of Rudolf Steiner.

The correspondence friendship continued to flourish between Marie von Sivers and Edouard Schuré. It is a special example of artistic exchange – music, literature, theatre – enlivened by deepest esoteric searching at the dawn of the Light Age. Soon Edouard Schuré, an avid reader, realized the spiritual significance of Rudolf Steiner. Also, he was one of the first to recognize the fact that Marie von Sivers' total support in everyday matters such as arranging trips and lectures, in artistic work as a great speech artist and as a serious and devoted esoteric pupil herself made Rudolf Steiner's blossoming mission feasible. When the official inauguration of the German Section of the Theosophical Society occurred, 18–21 October 1902, Rudolf Steiner mentioned in his opening address that Marie von Sivers would be his co-worker in the leadership of the Society, and, furthermore, through her recitations the artistic element would be represented[8]. Thus we experience from the beginning of Rudolf Steiner's work for a Society his intention to include artistic impulses.

Is history relevant for seekers of the spirit today?

For decades in the western world we have been living in an 'instant mode of civilization.' A sense for historical perspectives has diminished significantly, if not even in many instances totally disappeared. The reasons are legion and need not be enumerated. Perhaps we may notice today − after a century devoted to innumerable wars − a question dawning in various quarters: is humanity capable of learning anything from its experiences that can then become strong enough to avert similar disasters in the future? It will fall to the twenty-first century to wrestle with this question, or ultimately to self-destruct.

For the spiritual seeker there are certain laws that exert as significant an influence as do the laws of nature. One of these laws of the spirit we have already observed though Marie von Sivers' question to Rudolf Steiner at the Chrysanthemum Tea: to begin activity the initiate must wait until the appropriate question is placed. Marie von Sivers asked the initial question. Many such questions followed throughout the following years from other individuals that resulted in the development of eurythmy, of Waldorf School education, of anthroposophical medicine, of a Movement for Religious Renewal (The Christian Community) and of biodynamic agriculture, to cite but a few of the more visible examples. In retrospect one senses the greatness of the individuality who could place the initial karmic question to Rudolf Steiner that then unlocked the door to the twentieth century and allowed western Christian esotericism to enter in.

Another important spiritual law concerns the principle of continuity. Rudolf Steiner describes in his autobiography that whenever possible this principle must be observed. For this reason he linked onto the Theosophical Society while still maintaining his own spiritual independence until it became necessary to separate the work of his Esoteric School from the Esoteric School of Annie Besant in 1907 and then to form the Anthroposophical Society at Christmas 1912. This step resulted in a complete severing from the Theosophical Society with its Headquarters in Adyar.

The law of spiritual continuity finds its basis through a process of recognition. The degree of recognition will vary according to the evaluation of the spiritual legitimacy in each case. We find, for example, that, with the exception of Johann Wolfgang von Goethe, Rudolf Steiner probably mentions Helena Petrowna Blavatsky more than any other person. Indeed her greatness is perhaps seen more clearly through the eyes of Rudolf Steiner than in any other way and yet her limitations, in part resulting from the age in which she lived, also come into profile though his careful descriptions. Yet it was through her Theosophical Society that Rudolf Steiner found his first platform for esoteric lectures. For exoteric scientific and cultural lectures he had various prominent platforms, for example in Weimar and in Berlin.

For spiritual development today in the Light Age not only is it necessary to recognize the stream of continuity in which one must find one's spiritual bearings, but also the future, which radiates into the present, must be sensed. This is the great secret of the Akasha that Rudolf Steiner was able to reveal. For Edouard Schuré in September 1907 Rudolf Steiner formulated this law:

> At that time (1881) – and this already belongs to the external occult influences – I arrived at full clarity regarding the idea of time. This realization had no connection with my studies and it arose totally out of my occult life. It was the realization that there is a backwards-running evolution which interferes with the progressing one – the occult-astral knowledge of this is a requirement of supersensible vision.[9]

In summary we may conclude that particularly the *esoteric* seeker needs to develop an acute sense for the spiritual historical process. All karmic research demands this basic prerequisite.

Transition from the older mysteries to the new mysteries

Marie Steiner writes in an introduction to a 1939 edition of Edouard Schuré's *The Sacred Drama of Eleusis,* which she had translated into German in 1906 and Rudolf Steiner then transformed into a free rhythmic form:

> In May 1906 the first meeting between Edouard Schuré and Rudolf Steiner occurred. He characterized it as a high point of his life. And whoever is surprised by this ... [whoever] saw in his eyes how he recognized him again, this lighting up as if from deep shafts of memory and this joyful comprehension of words which were inhaled by him as something which was yearned for, anticipated, and desired, he could experience, that a destiny-meeting had occurred ... Prior to this meeting there had been a correspondence already for seven years between me [Marie Steiner] which had brought Schuré's being – humanly speaking – closer to us. I experienced him [Schuré] for the first time in the flesh and knew that here a pupil had recognized his teacher.[10]

From this description by Marie Steiner we fathom how this meeting reflects a karmic friendship between these three individualities stemming from older Mystery School times. Surely this constellation occurring at the beginning of the New Age must stand in a prominent light in the Akasha Chronicle. Immediately a co-operative artistic–esoteric work started between the three that led to the performance of Edouard Schuré's *Sacred Drama of Eleusis* at the Congress of the Theosophical Society in Munich at Whitsuntide 1907. Marie von Sivers played the main role as Demeter and Rudolf Steiner directed the entire artistic form of the Congress.

Between the destiny meeting in May 1906 and the Munich Congress in May 1907, which was the decisive turning point esoterically and artistically for Rudolf Steiner's task that from then on bore an esoteric Christian signature connected with the individuality of Christian Rosenkreutz, a singular event occurred on 17 December 1906. From the vantage point of a ninety-year retrospect one may interpret the meeting and collaboration of the three at that particular moment as a spiritual prerequisite necessary for a new step. The impress of this step appears in a lecture at Christmas in Berlin known in English as *Signs and Symbols of the Christmas Festival,* in which Rudolf Steiner describes at the outset his intention to bring his listeners to a deeper understanding of the being of the sun. Then follows:

> We will now hear those words, which reflect the deepest meaning of the Christmas Mystery. The words resounded for the devoutly listening pupils of the Mysteries though all times, before they themselves were allowed to enter into the Mysteries.[11]

One would imagine after the earnestness of this orientation that Rudolf Steiner would then speak the words himself. Not so, however; Marie von Sivers in her uniquely artistically formed speech then recited:

> Behold the Sun
> At the midnight hour!
> In the lifeless ground
> Build your rocky bower!
> So, when in depths you mourn,
> Find you in Death's dark night
> Creation's pulse new-born
> With living Morning Light.
> The Powers on high make known
> The eternal Word Divine;
> The Deeps must guard their own –
> Peace, in their sacred shrine.
> In gloom you live –
> Create anew a Sun!

> In matter weave —
> Know Spirit-bliss begun!

This verse is the first verse composed in rhymed form by Rudolf Steiner. He describes further then in the lecture how the initiates from all Mystery Schools — the Egyptian, the Eleusinian, the Babylonian–Chaldaean, the Indian Brahman and so on — led their pupils to an experience of the sun at the midnight hour.

The event of 17 December 1906 represents a transition moment from the older Mysteries into the new Mysteries. These mantric words brought into modern human language by Rudolf Steiner resounded before human beings openly through the voice of Marie von Sivers, through her recitation. Thus the art of formed speech builds a bridge to the new Mysteries. It is a mystery itself how the larynx of this special individuality could bring to manifestation words from the ancient mysteries so that they could receive an incarnation possibility. Rudolf Steiner brings them out of the Akasha, forms them anew and guides them to the threshold of our time, but then he lets them enter into the stream of time through artistic recitation. This event marks the beginning of a unique union of esotericism and art through the collaboration of Rudolf Steiner and Marie von Sivers. This union remains a characteristic cornerstone for the work of anthroposophy right into the present time. In rapid succession from that December 1906 event onwards a new life for art inspired by Rudolf Steiner's spiritual science unfolded. In Chapter 34 of *The Story of My Life* we read:

> In the Theosophical Society artistic interests were scarcely fostered at all. From a certain point of view this situation was at that time quite intelligible ... The members of such a society centre all their interests at first upon the reality of the spiritual life. In the sense-world man appears to them only in his transitory existence severed from the spiritual. Art seems to them to have its activity within this severed existence ... [and] to be apart from the spiritual reality for which they seek. Because this was so in the Theosophical

Society, artists did not feel at home there. To Marie von Sivers and to me it was important to also enliven the artistic within the Society. Spiritual knowledge as an experience takes hold of the whole human existence. All the forces of the soul are stimulated. Into formative fantasy the light of spirit experience shines when this experience is present ... Marie von Sivers had her place in the art of word-formation; she had a most beautiful relationship to dramatic presentation. Thus for anthroposophy a field of art was there in which the fruitfulness of spiritual perception for art might be tested.

New mysteries and new art impulses

The end of Kali Yuga after 5000 years and the advent of the Light Age will perhaps be viewed from future perspectives as manifesting most clearly and dramatically through art in the fourteen years before the outbreak of World War I. Not only great innovations such as in painting, music, sculpture, dance and theatre announce the experience of crossing the threshold into spirit realms, but also the destiny meetings that enhanced the new streams of creativity are of singular importance. Kandinsky and Schoenberg may be mentioned as representatives for the many deep and fateful friendships in art that mark this period. They are a generation of spiritual seekers who incarnated with art as their gift of destiny and their means of expression.

Directly in the middle of these fourteen years of relative international peace and spiritual–cultural receptivity, the Munich Congress of the Theosophical Society took place. Rudolf Steiner, Marie von Sivers and members in Munich planned and carried this Congress, which introduced totally new elements into the life of the Theosophical Society. It rapidly engendered, as Marie Steiner described it later, a 'separation of souls' *(Seelenentscheidung)*. As the documents pertaining to the Congress are not yet easily accessible in English we will take note of various basic — however by no means comprehensive — aspects.

Several months before the Congress the programme, which was printed in English and German, was sent to the members. Basic points could be mentioned ahead of time as orientation, such as:

> The content of the presentations will arise from lectures springing from the theosophical world-view, artistic presentations and purely social gatherings ... The artistic presentations will be chosen so that in the area of sculptural as well as musical and poetic art, the specifics will form a harmonious whole with the theosophical world-conception. Therefore in one of the events also the attempt will be made through drama to give a presentation of a Mystery. [that is, Schuré's *Sacred Drama of Eleusis*].[12]

Rudolf Steiner's and Marie von Sivers' spiritual intention for this Congress sounds clearly here:

> It would be very desirable, even if only in a modest framework, if it could for once be demonstrated how the theosophical world-conception is capable of enlivening the artistic sphere ... so that Theosophy need not remain only a sum total of theoretical viewpoints, but rather can experience transformation into the sensory–visual and the perceptible appropriate to the mood. In this way it [Theosophy] indeed can work fructifying upon the rest of culture.[13]

And this indeed inspired many of the over 600 members present, but it also was incomprehensible and even repulsive for others.

We may imagine their shock when they entered the conference hall and saw that all of the walls were a brilliant red! To this Rudolf Steiner wrote in his report for the journal *Lucifer-Gnosis:*

> Esoteric knowledge says: 'If you wish to attune yourself in your most inward nature, as the gods were attuned when

they bestowed the green plant covering [on the earth], then learn to endure 'red' in your surroundings as they [the gods] also had to do ... the genuine esotericist when he represents the two opposite entities of the creative world foundation in occult symbolism, interprets the green below as a characteristic sign of the earthly and the red above as a sign of the heavenly (Elohim) creative forces.[14]

On the side walls and at the back there were the seven apocalyptic seals designed by Rudolf Steiner and executed in colour by Clara Rettich. Rudolf Steiner took great pains to explain that they were not merely symbolic in nature but much more, as they represent certain objective experiences in the astral world:

One should experience the content of these seven pictures with one's entire soul and undivided feeling [original German, *Gemüt*], one should shape within oneself, in one's soul, the content as it lives in form and colour, so that it lives inwardly in one's Imagination.[15]

In connection with these seals Rudolf Steiner now reveals that what until 1907 had been strictly preserved by spiritual guardians as absolutely secret now must be made accessible to the public. This is demanded for the further development of spiritual life in our time. And further:

A column was placed each time between two seals. The seven columns could not be formed sculpturally, rather as a substitute they had to be painted. However they are conceived as real architectural forms and correspond to the 'seven columns' of the 'true Rosicrucian temple' ... the capitals of these columns represent the planetary development of our earth system ... in the forms of these capitals the inner life of each one of the development stages comes to expression [that is, Saturn, Sun, Moon, Earth, Jupiter, Venus, Vulcan].[16]

Even through sparse descriptions we realize today that what took place during those few days comprises spiritual impulses out of deepest Christian esotericism in its indivisible connection with art, which, as seed impulses, were then planted a few years later into the form and colours of the First Goetheanum. The First Goetheanum should have at least spanned the twentieth century but its task as far as physical accessibility is concerned was abruptly terminated by fire on 31 December 1922. In the Congress hall in Munich aspects of the Mysteries were placed before the participants right into the mysteries of the blood. In the front of the hall there were two columns, the one red, the other deep blue–red. They indicate the 'Mystery of Humanity's Development' (Rudolf Steiner).

> Occult science inscribes four deeply significant sayings upon these two columns. When the human soul meditatively enters into these four sayings, then out of their depths comprehensive cosmic and human secrets well forth.[17]

> ### Jachin and Boaz
> J
> In pure Thinking you do find
> The Self that can hold itself.
> Transmute the Thought into Picture-life
> And you will know creative Wisdom.
> B
> Condense your Feeling into Light:
> Formative powers are revealed through you.
> Forge your Will into deeds of Being:
> So shall you share in World-creation.[18]

A most important signature of this Congress stands in full revelation on the programme booklet itself. In the same report in *Lucifer-Gnosis* Rudolf Steiner offers an explanation that has far-reaching significance. Whereas these aspects were familiar to the more intimate esoteric students in the Esoteric School of the Theosophical Society as of 1903, here they enter openly into the cultural scene. The programme was also red. On the outside leaf in the upper left corner in a blue oval was a black cross entwined by red roses. Then to the right of the cross the letters:

> E. D. N – I.C.M. – P.S.S.R. These are the ten beginning alphabet letters of the words, through which through art true Rosicrucianism is summarized in one objective: 'Ex deo nascimur, in Christo morimur, per spiritum sanctum reviviscimus.' [From God we are born, in Christ we die, through the Holy Spirit we resurrect]. The cross symbol entwined by roses expresses esoterically the meaning of Rosicrucianism.[19]

In the Congress hall rented for the meeting and transformed by the red walls, the apocalyptic seals, the seven painted columns with their capitals and the red column and the blue one, the words of Schuré's Sacred Eleusis drama sounded. The echoes of ancient Mystery wisdom translated and formed appropriately for early twentieth century consciousness by Marie von Sivers and Rudolf Steiner streamed into a modern contemporary setting, which was in harmony with a Christian Rosenkreutz task for our time; namely, the conscious union of a Christ–Michael-centred esotericism with expression in art, which evolves out of the trinitarian stream represented in the ten letters.

Glimpses of the script of destiny after the Munich Congress

Marie Steiner described this time, as was mentioned before, as the separation of souls. This was indeed the case, for the spiritual consequences went far deeper than the Congress programme itself. In an Esoteric Lesson for pupils of the Esoteric School immediately after the Munich Congress on 1 June 1907, Rudolf Steiner refers to the Esoteric School under the guidance of Annie Besant and his own Esoteric School, which he had led since 1904. Both were within the framework of the Theosophical Society:

> Until now both Schools were united in a large circle under the common leadership of the Masters.[20] Now, however, the Western School has made itself independent and there are now two Schools standing next to each other; the one in the East, the other in the West; two smaller circles instead of the one large [circle]. The Eastern School will be led by Mrs Annie Besant, and whoever in his heart feels more drawn to her, he can no longer remain in our School. Each one should exactly examine which way the longing of his heart leads him. At the summit of our Western School there are two Masters: Master Jesus and Master Christian Rosenkreutz. And on two paths they lead us, the Christian path and the Christian–Rosicrucian path ...[21]

As we have seen the latter path is inseparably connected with art. In 1910 the first Mystery Drama was performed in Munich: *The Portal of Initiation. A Rosicrucian Mystery,* followed each year by a subsequent drama – four in all – until the war broke out. Marie Steiner played the central role of Maria. As of 1912 eurythmy entered through special karmic circumstances into anthroposophical life, and was developed mutually by Rudolf Steiner and Marie Steiner; the Goetheanum building, 'the House of the Word' was artistically conceived and shaped and thus Marie Steiner's art of formed speech had a home at last. A rich artistic life could unfold because Rudolf Steiner himself was also an outstanding artist. This fact is often taken for granted; however, to gain an accurate appreciation and evaluation one may look at other highly developed spiritual teachers from the point of view of creative artistic productivity. They do not keep pace with Rudolf Steiner. True to the Rosicrucian trinitarian impulse all branches of life touched by anthroposophy could become 'art,' thus the art of education, the art of healing, even the art of agriculture could develop.

This transforming quality of Rosicrucian spiritual–scientific esotericism and art prepared the spiritual soul–soil of the human beings whose destiny led them to Rudolf Steiner and Marie von Sivers-Steiner so that when impulses from the supersensible Michael School could be brought to manifestation on the earth through Rudolf Steiner in the Christmas Foundation Meeting of the General Anthroposophical Society,[22] the hearts of those present were well prepared to be receptive. Then with the development of the School of Spiritual Science in its esoteric work as well as in the work of the various professional Sections the Rosicrucian soul-culture could meet the Michaelic spirit-culture. This development continues into our time as a working manifestation of the New Mysteries.

Consequences for the twenty-first century

In this brief consideration of the first seven-year period of Rudolf Steiner's and Marie von Sivers-Steiner's spiritual–artistic collaboration certain aspects evidence not only a personal configuration but also an archetypal one. Their validity may serve as guidelines in a world that often demonstrates pervasive confusion in spiritual matters. A profusion of esoteric paths exists today, which verifies that innumerable people are seeking spiritual orientation. Now a century into the Light Age this belongs to contemporary life and is well beyond the initial thrusts across the threshold into the supersensible world that we referred to with the artists in the early years of the twentieth century. What may serve as karmic indicators today that a destiny configuration truly contains possibilities that surpass the purely personal level? At least seven aspects may be extrapolated from our considerations. Their sequence is of secondary importance, with the exception of the first aspect, which simply stated is: What is the nature of the initial quest? For Marie von Sivers-Steiner it was: *'Où trouver la vérité?*[23] Secondly, which human encounters during the quest provide bridges to other destiny meetings and to guidance in the quest itself? We have seen the unique correspondence-meeting between Marie von Sivers and Edouard Schuré and its far-reaching consequences even today for us inasmuch as we have formed a connection with anthroposophy.

A third consideration may not surface so easily for inspection as in the case of Rudolf Steiner and Marie von Sivers-Steiner: who asks the decisive question that enables new spiritual and thus also new social dimensions to enter the stage of contemporary life? In a more modest way each seeker at some time has a 'Chrysanthemum Tea,' only he may let it slip by unnoticed.

Then the moment arrives when the seeker becomes aware of the spiritual necessity of continuity. Today this takes on important new dimensions due to the superabundance of occult groups. We do well to ask: what is the background, what is the stream, what is the 'spiritual pedigree' behind the guru or group?

These questions lead to a fifth consideration that centres around the evaluation of the historical moment in which one stands. What can one sense coming towards one from the future? Rudolf Steiner's awareness of future spiritual necessities streamed into the work for the Munich Congress, for example. The result was a new direction for western Christian spirituality and now this movement encompasses more people and activities than can be enumerated.

For our time and into the future a great question concerns the 'word' in the most extended sense. How does art speak today? Does it emerge and receive its inspiration from a spirituality that furthers the development of the human being or is it yet another fetter to the physical world because it lacks the forces of transformation that lead to resurrection. Art springing from the impulses of Rudolf Steiner and Marie Steiner lead the human being to discover the latent art within his own nature. It is a task connected with the New Mysteries that each human being once again discovers art as a bridge to the spirit, not in the mediumistic manner of older times but through wide-awake consciousness.

A seventh consideration is that of true spiritual, artistic and social collaboration. As humanity evolves further this aspect becomes increasingly essential. Even Rudolf Steiner in the greatness of his spiritual stature worked in our age in connection with other people. We have gained a glimpse into the most essential collaboration that continued also after Rudolf Steiner's death. For the twenty-three years that were granted to Marie Steiner she tirelessly worked artistically for the further development of speech formation, of drama at the Second Goetheanum, of eurythmy and for the editing and publishing of Rudolf Steiner's works. There were many other competent and faithful co-workers as well at the various stages of Rudolf Steiner's life work. They cannot be mentioned within the limits of this article, however for us the message is clear. The present time and the future raying into this epoch demand that human beings work together irrespective of the degree of spiritual development they may represent. Rudolf Steiner and Marie Steiner responded to this demand in an exemplary manner as their work unfolded first in theosophical circles and then within the Anthroposophical Society. It demonstrates for all who wish to plunge beneath the surface that the highest art, the so-called royal art, will be the social art.

References

1. Extensive biographical research has been undertaken by Hella Wiesberger and published by the Rudolf Steiner Verlag 1988, Dornach: *Marie Steiner-von Sivers. Ein Leben für die Anthroposophie.* These studies as well as the Collected Writings of Marie Steiner (two volumes) are not yet available in English translation. For biographical material refer to Savitch, Marie, *Marie Steiner-von Sivers. Fellow Worker with Rudolf Steiner,* Rudolf Steiner Press, London 1967.
2. From a letter of 23 August 1948 to Simone Coroze-Rihouët in Paris, in Wiesberger, Hella, *Marie Steiner-von Sivers. Ein Leben für die Anthroposophie. Eine biographische Dokumentation,* Rudolf Steiner Verlag, Dornach 1988, p.69. Translation into English, Virginia Sease with permission of Hella Wiesberger, Rudolf Steiner Verlag.
3. Ibid. p.69.
4. Ibid. p.75.

5. Ibid. p.77.
6. Steiner, Rudolf, lecture on 11 October 1915 in *The Occult Movement in the Nineteenth Century and Its Relation to Modern Culture.* Rudolf Steiner Press, London 1973.
7. Mücke, Johanna, *'Aus der Geschichte des Philosophisch-Anthroposophischen Verlags'* in the journal *Die Menschenschule,* March 1942, also in *Marie Steiner im Zeugnis von Tatjana Kisseleff, Johanna Mücke, Walter Abendroth, Ernst von Schenk,* Basle 1984.
8. See Scholl, Mathilde, *Zum 20. Oktober 1902 und 1932* in *'Was in der Anthroposophischen Gesellschaft vorgeht,'* 1932, No. 43/44.
9. Rudolf Steiner/Marie von Sivers, *Correspondence and Documents 1901–1925.* (GA 262) Tr. C. von Arnim. Rudolf Steiner Press and Anthroposophic Press, London and New York 1988. (The Barr Document at the beginning of the book.)
10. Steiner, Marie, *Gesammelte Schriften II: Rudolf Steiner und die Redenden Künste,* ed. Edwin Froböse, Rudolf Steiner-Nachlassverwaltung, Dornach, Switzerland 1974, p.321.
11. Steiner, Rudolf, Lecture of 17 December 1906 in *Signs and Symbols of the Christmas Festival,* Anthroposophic Press, 1969.
12. Steiner, Rudolf, *Bilder okkulter Siegel und Säulen. Der Münchner Kongress Pfingsten 1907 und seine Auswirkungen.* Rudolf Steiner Verlag, Dornach, Switzerland 1993, p.25.
13. *Ibid.*
14. Steiner, Rudolf, *'Der theosophische Kongress von 1907'* in *Lucifer Gnosis,* Rudolf Steiner Verlag, Dornach 1987, p.593.
15. Ibid. p.594.
16. Ibid. p.600.
17. Ibid. p.602.
18. Steiner, Rudolf, *Verses and Meditations,* Rudolf Steiner Press, Bristol 1993, with an introduction and notes by George Adams. See especially reference 4, p.227 for further elucidation.
19. See reference 17.
20. After 1914 Rudolf Steiner gradually dropped the designation 'Master' and spoke of Leaders of humanity, or Teachers of humanity.
21. Steiner, Rudolf, *Zur Geschichte und aus den Inhalten der ersten Abteilung der Esoterischen Schule 1904–1914.* Rudolf Steiner Verlag, Dornach 1984, p.329.
22. Steiner, Rudolf, *The Christmas Conference for the Foundation of the General Anthroposophical Society 1923–1924,* Anthroposophic Press, New York 1990.
23. See reference 2.

Karma research

Nick Thomas

'Other peoples' problems mostly seem so much easier to solve than *mine*! My problems do not seem sufficiently important to others ...'

In one way such a view seems trivial and absurd, yet for all that it reveals something interesting, for the law of my life is the law of *my life*, not yours. It is an individual law, unlike, say, the law of gravity, which is general. We tend to think of general laws somewhat spatially, applying to a complete domain *at once*, so that all objects on earth experience gravity. We include time only in the sense that this is an enduring law, so gravity is supposed to have been as valid for Julius Caesar as it is for me, as it will be for future generations. We do not normally think of a law that operates *actually in time itself*, being valid for a sequence of events but not for other sequences running parallel in space. Yet my karma has this quality, for it is not your karma, and it operates through the sequence of my lives.

But surely Rudolf Steiner's research into karma revealed laws applicable to all? If my thinking is weak in one life I will have a weak will in the next, and vice versa. If I am male in one life I am likely to be female in the next. If I am egotistic in one life I may suffer from malaria in the next. Many, many such laws and examples were discovered by Steiner, with a general character. We encounter here the weaving between the generic and the individual. If we take the sum total of generic qualities of a person: height, build, national characteristics, sex and so on, is anything left if they are all removed? Materialistic psychology thinks not. Likewise, if we remove all the results of karma such as predisposition to illness, detailed physical characteristics, temperament, talents and capacities, the balance (or otherwise) of the soul forces, all that is of a generic quality, is anything left? If so, what?

What is left is the core individual *to whom* all these things happen. If a fence near a golf course repeatedly gets struck by golf balls, it may become dented or partially broken, but it learns nothing. Externally inflicted changes do not create individuality, so a fence does not become in any meaningful way individual. Such events only have significance if they happen to a core individuality that learns and is inwardly changed by them. The generic laws within which an individual struggles and learns are woven around him. Clearly outer general laws such as gravity are there for all alike but even then we find that different individuals can have distinct relationships to those laws: some are irritated by them and seek to circumvent them, some love them, some find them easy to master, others find them hard to accommodate. The generic laws of karma are much more closely bound to the individual, teaching special lessons which that individual needs. *This* weaving is much more of an individual matter, for it only has meaning *for an individual*. The individual law is then that which weaves the generic and it is a law in the sense that it serves the developmental needs of the individual in an effective and wise manner, indeed in a loving manner. It is not, as even a superficial observation of life shows, sentimental. Love is not sentimentality and seems to be most stern, yet is loving in that the experiences it brings to an individual are those most needed in order to progress, that is, are for the individual's greatest benefit.

Research into karma thus involves two major levels, the discovery of the general laws at work and the much harder to find karmic threads of destiny of individuals. Why should I or any other be permitted to look into the latter? The former do not carry the same moral overtones and seem more suited to research. We need here to free the term 'research' from a one-sided idea that it only has to do with what is scientific. It will only be effective if conducted in a scientific manner but its subject need not be 'the stuff science' as it were. It must also involve art and the greatest possible reverence. For the way the destiny of individuals is woven, sometimes grand, sometimes tragic, sometimes to bestow blessing, is clearly a very exalted art. What an individual needs is provided neither by recipe nor rote but is an individual creation in each case, a mighty artistic 'solution,' even if involving general ingredients. Consequently, no research method can hope to unravel such a creation that, itself, involves no art, for the perceived and the perceiver must needs share some common ground. The highest beings of the hierarchies exercise this art and themselves live through our lives in advance. Not to be shaken to the core of one's being by such a fact is unthinkable. Life does not follow karmic tramlines and we experience different possible ways to go, with real decisions to be made, and we encounter a number of karmic communities to which we belong. We cannot pursue them all, yet all are real possibilities. So those beings must have *lived through them all,* not just the actual course of life we eventually follow.

Spiritual research involves both perception and thinking, and it is distinguished from ordinary scientific research by the need to undergo self-development to attain the possibility of having new percepts and being in a position to frame the quite new thoughts appropriate to them. In addition, a moral development is required to provide the basis for a confidence in what is unveiled. What is the good of new percepts if they are of uncertain merit? Mere bravado, such as is sometimes encountered among those who go into these matters superficially, leads in the end only to confusion. Moral forces are laws of the spiritual world that give the same sure ground to the researcher as do the laws of Nature in the sense world. Without them we literally 'fall to the ground' of the sense world (in the least unfortunate case).

In the lectures Rudolf Steiner gave on *Karmic Relationships* in 1924 he carefully describes case studies he made, which both reveal the workings of karma and provide a detailed description of the spiritual research methods he used. In one case he had great difficulty in tracing the karma of an individual to previous lives, and in the end the way the man blew his nose provided the needed link! Here we see a striking example of just how individual these matters are, for at first such a thing might seem trivial. Yet so complete is the artistic weaving of the fabric of our lives that the whole is expressed in every detail. Further, in each case the appropriate link must be found and, although general techniques are developed, they really serve as a guide towards that observation in the individual case which is decisive. An example of a more general trend in evolution is the metamorphosis of the culture of the Arabic peoples a millennium ago into the style of natural science today, Charles Darwin being an example of a former military general in that culture who carried over into his scientific work a metamorphosis of both his achievements and failures at that time. Such broad trends give a general background within which related individual cases may more easily be traced. Conversely, it is clear that broad trends are also uncovered through the workings of individual karma, which serve as pointers. Outstanding figures in history carry world karma as well as their own, and to that extent may more readily be traced. The relationship of Marx and Engels is instructive here, for the social impulses they bore within them – no matter the way they were taken up – were grounded in a social problem between the two of them in a previous life, where the one ousted the other from his property.

A further remarkable fact was uncovered by Steiner, namely that in some cases the Akashic record pertaining to particular cases was apparently 'blank.' Further investigation revealed that they concerned incidents that had been forgiven by Christ and for which the record had been 'erased.' In reality, such records are only available to Christian initiates, that is, to those who receive the new form of initiation instituted by Christ that supersedes the now decadent form of initiation of the old mysteries. This has nothing to do with religion, being concerned with objective spiritual processes available in principle to all on the earth. It does indicate that research into karma will increasingly only be reliably founded on the basis of such processes, without which only dubious results are obtainable.

This leads us back to the question as to why research into these deep and, indeed, holy matters should be possible at all. One reason is simply that it is needed now. For example, in the fields of medicine and education a genuine insight into the karma of a patient or a difficult child can be very beneficial in giving effective and appropriate help. Such insight is generally only granted to those who actually need it, that is, to the doctor or teacher who has genuine responsibility for the case. The taking of responsibility provides the 'guarantee' needed by the spiritual powers concerned, which is absent when we are merely curious. It is an example of the fact that modern spiritual research is not a 'cloister' activity but rather is conducted in the real stream of life. The other aspect of the qualification needed for such research concerns the fact mentioned in the previous paragraph: that the motive for the work needs to be rooted in the Christian stream of initiation, even if the researcher is not an initiate as such. This will lend added reliability to what is uncovered. Finally, we must remark that merely general laws or 'rules' are also insufficient here and there may be sound karmic reasons why a particular individual is able to conduct research into karma that may not be obvious to others.

Intimations in images

Nothart M. Rohlfs

It is only the smallest part of what shapes the destiny of the human being that appears to the ordinary waking consciousness. The remainder generally operates in the unconscious. Yet it is precisely in revealing what belongs to destiny that one can see how what is unconscious can be brought into consciousness. Those who speak of what is at present unconscious as if it must remain absolutely in the realm of the unknown, and as if it represented a kind of boundary to human knowledge, are quite wrong. With every aspect of his own destiny that reveals itself to the human being, he is raising something previously unconscious up into consciousness.[1]

When the unconscious can thus become conscious, images are called forth in the soul that have the character of memories, but cannot be related to one's present biography. In these it seems also that destiny reveals itself from the depths of the unconscious.

In this article we shall attempt, on the basis of many conversations and of my own experiences, briefly to determine the conditions under which such imaginative experiences occur. The phenomena we shall isolate to enable them to be recognized individually do not normally appear separately in the reality of life, but are generally in combination with other elements.

The strongest feelings and impulses of will, such as love and hate, have their sources in the unconscious regions referred to above. These sources themselves are human destiny, karma. Each of us becomes aware of them to begin with in our encounters with other people. The impulses of will and the feelings that have their roots in destiny play into these encounters.

What takes place in the soul encounter of two lovers raises them above the level of their everyday existence. The loved one can thus be experienced not merely as the result of past destiny but also in his orientation towards his own ideals for the future. Something of his future being shines out as if what he wishes to become in the future were already fully present today. Our love for another human being thus allows us to see into the future, and there to perceive what alone can make comprehensible the present condition of the human being, the nature and direction of his path through life. The lover heightens and expands the receptivity of his soul, and the loved one becomes more beautiful, richer and more perfect in the love that is brought towards him. His soul reveals itself in the depths of this love.

In 1923, Rudolf Steiner spoke of a process that seems surprisingly similar to what has been described. In connection with the central task of anthroposophy, a renewal of human community from out of the spirit, he speaks of an 'awakening of the human being in the spiritual and soul qualities of the other.' As far as the soul and spiritual qualities that appear in this way are concerned, this awakening, it seems to me, might be described very much in the same words that were used above to indicate the transformation that the loved one experiences in the love that is brought towards him or that the lover experiences in the capacity for love that is developed within him.

The central difference between the two may be that we are graced with the love for each other by destiny, whereas the process of awakening in the encounter with each other has to be learned consciously, and on our own initiative. If we succeed in this, it can become a foundation of a new community life, the foundation stone of an anthroposophy that has its roots in human communities. Steiner himself speaks of it in this way:

This need has simply been a very basic one since the beginning of the twentieth century, and will become stronger and stronger. This need will become apparent throughout the twentieth century despite its chaotic, tumultuous character which will affect the whole of civilisation: the need will be felt for human beings to achieve a higher degree of awakening in the encounter with each other than can be experienced merely in the encounter with our natural surroundings. Dreamlife is awakened by natural surroundings to day waking consciousness. Day time consciousness is awakened by other human beings, by their soul and spirit qualities to a higher consciousness. The human being must become more for the other than heretofore. We must become awakening beings for each other. Human beings must get closer to one another than ever before: everyone who encounters another must become an awakening being for him. The modern human being who has come into life at this time has stored up far too much karma not to feel connected by his destiny with everyone whom he encounters in life. If one looks back to previous ages, when souls were younger, they had fewer karmic connections. Now it is simply a matter of necessity that we are not only awakened by nature but also by the human beings with whom we are karmically connected, and whom we seek out.[2]

With regard to the necessary conditions for a true understanding of anthroposophy, he says in another lecture:

We only begin to develop an initial understanding of the spiritual world when we awaken to the spirit and soul qualities of the other human being. Only then do we begin to have a real understanding of anthroposophy. Indeed, it behoves us to take this condition as a starting point for a true understanding of anthroposophy, which one could call:

the awakening of the human being by the spirit and soul qualities of the other.[3]

Rudolf Steiner makes a few opening remarks about the conditions applying to such a higher awakening. Thus, for example, he speaks of a 'spiritual idealism' which would have to be 'planted' in human communities. But he says very little about the nature of the awakening itself.

In my experience, this awakening in the encounter with the other feels, to the one who awakes, like the unexpected sharing in a kind of blossoming of the other: as if one's own individuality were more strongly present in the physical condition, thus giving it a kind of bloom. The person opposite even appears to the eyes of the beholder more physically beautiful, fresher, stronger and more individual (his features seem to become firmer, to take on clearer outlines, to become harmonious). He seems visibly 'to blossom.' One could also say, to penetrate his own physical form more fully, to make use of its potential more comprehensively, more strongly and with more presence of mind.

This 'blossoming' has its counterpart in the simultaneous heightening of the consciousness of the person concerned, who is involved both in producing and perceiving it.

In my experience, this awakening in the encounter with the spiritual and soul qualities of the other human being represents a process that may precede the appearance of pictures in the soul that have the character of memory as described.

As if they came out of this 'blossoming,' pictorial impressions may arise in the soul of the one who awakens, which appear like delicate, imaginative shapes around the other human being. These may take the form of human figures or faces, of simple or detailed scenes that seem, nevertheless, not to relate to events belonging to the present life.

It may be that such 'scenes' occupy one's full attention, although they do so without one's losing awareness of outer sense impressions or ordinary, everyday consciousness. These impressions actually appear rather more in such a way that the underlying condition of soul in which they make their appearance resembles that of concentrated reflection on something which is difficult to remember, and which is just occurring to one. One makes a certain effort to bring the forgotten fact before one's inner gaze. As we know, this does not mean that the sense world disappears from one's consciousness but rather that it fades into the background, like something of lesser importance that one takes for granted.

If awakening in the encounter of the spirit and soul qualities of the other human being may be termed a kind of fundamental precondition for imaginative karmic experience, then two further elements should be described which have the same character.

Let me give an example of the second element. We all know the situation where we are at a gathering or a conference where we are 'exposed' to a speaker whom we have already frequently met, and for whose utterances we are unable, even with the best will in the world, to arouse in ourselves the slightest interest. It may even go so far that we are seized by a strong and recurring antipathy as soon as the person concerned opens his mouth. One day we may decide no longer to force ourselves, against all our inclinations, to listen to the man. We accept, as it were for the time being, our inability to take an interest in him, or his thoughts, via the spoken word. Instead of this, on the other hand, we make a serious effort to find another way of approaching the person to gain access to him by a different route.

My own experience of such an occasion occurred during a lecture when I stopped trying to listen to the words being spoken. My concern to meet the speaker somehow or other, despite my antipathy, directed my attention to the movements of his arms and then his hands. Eventually, I became absolutely riveted by the movements of his fingers which had a fascinating effect on me. It seemed as if what the person had to say always flowed into a kind of pointed, sabre-like, energetically executed, even flame-like movement of his fingers, as if the concentrated essence of what he said flowed towards them, and from them on into the surroundings, working on into them. While I was engrossed in this process, there appeared before the speaker the image of a person who had absolutely nothing in common with him, but which, nevertheless, had an almost shattering effect on me. The predominant impression was of a face which belonged to an historical figure of the nineteenth century known to me from photographs. Immediately, the thought occurred to me: 'Should there be anything to this (in the form of a connection of some kind, or indeed, of the two individualities being identical), then the step from the previous incarnation to the present would be a truly astonishing and admirable one.'

The feelings that followed on from this thought showed the person concerned in a completely different light compared with the way I had experienced him before.

What is important here is only the phenomenon that occurred, and the 'response' of the soul. No claims will be made in respect of anything else. There is no question of asserting that this constitutes a case of reincarnation validated by spiritual science. The example is only intended to show that phenomena of this kind are occurring more and more frequently today, and that the soul, given that it is familiar with the appropriate concepts, may easily incline to interpret what it sees in connection with previous incarnations, and that the phenomena seem to be the result of a more than usually intense observation of the trivia and minor details of everyday life.

Rudolf Steiner says of such a heightened attentiveness towards the otherwise unremarkable impressions of life, that it could lead relatively quickly to the development of an apprehension of karmic connections. Could it be that a consciousness of everyday things, heightened by practice, could develop into the faculty of directing one's attention accurately to what is significant, and that such a condition of soul could be more receptive to karmic impressions?

A third element should be mentioned here that seems also to be a prerequisite for the appearance of pictorial impressions connected with previous earthly lives.

It is often experienced that images of this kind also appear in connection with overcoming an inner resistance that has its roots in personal relationships. The following might occur, for example: during the course of ordinary working life, someone is asked to take on a particular task that involves other colleagues. An inexplicable aversion arises in him, growing stronger all the time, which seems to have to do with the colleagues, although it does not seem to relate to any particular experiences he may have had with them. Despite his massive reluctance to do so, the person decides to take on the task in question. The determining factor is a clear feeling that, despite all the obvious counter-arguments, this is the right way forward.

Carrying out the task turns out to be no easier than he feared. The social interaction does not turn out to be easy. Nevertheless, the effort is made to bring what has been taken on to a successful conclusion. Then it might happen that, in a specific work situation, something comes before the soul quite unexpectedly in the form of memory pictures of events that seem to relate to other circumstances and other times. At the same time, one can have the feeling that one 'knows' exactly who the people are today who appear in these recollections. Later on, one might have the surprising impression that one has received something like an explanation for the inner reluctance one has experienced by means of images apparently deriving from previous incarnations.

Also in respect of this third element, Rudolf Steiner has made remarks that can shed an extraordinarily interesting light on the relationship between opposition one experiences in life, and the apprehension of a karmic background to them.[4]

For reasons of brevity, no reference has yet been made to the possibilities and requirements of investigating and testing this kind of 'non' sense impression referred to above. Naturally there is the greatest need for meticulous, spiritual scientific investigation and testing of such soul phenomena in order to learn to gauge their reality and to avoid falling prey to error and illusion.

More and more frequently today, impressions appear before the soul under circumstances such as those described, which seem to be recollections of previous earth lives or of people who were alive before. In my experience, the circumstances in which they appear fall into broadly three categories:

1. an awakening in the encounter with the spirit and soul qualities of the other human being;

2. a heightened attentiveness to the minor details of life;

3. the overcoming of inner resistance which has its origins in personal relationships.

These three elements which appear as it were in the 'biographical foreground' of such experiences, seem to have an inner connection with the threefold transformation and heightening of the will, the powers of cognition, and one's feeling power of soul:

3. a conscious taking hold of the will = overcoming resistance;

2. a conscious taking hold of one's powers of cognition = increased attentiveness and heightened consciousness;

1. a conscious taking hold of the central powers of the human soul = awakening in the encounter with the other.

The elements that Rudolf Steiner refers to frequently in connection with exercises of the soul seem to be appearing here in their first beginnings and in a metamorphosed way in biographical situations. Are we seeing here what were formerly the principles of initiation now appearing in nascent form as the principles of civilization?

References

1. Steiner, Rudolf, *Anthroposophical Leading Thoughts* (GA 26), number 47. Rudolf Steiner Press, London 1973.
2. Steiner, Rudolf, *Awakening to Community* (GA 257), Dornach 3.3.23. Anthroposophic Press 1974.
3. Ibid. Stuttgart 27.2.23.
4. Steiner, Rudolf, *Reincarnation and Karma* (GA 135), particularly Berlin 30.1.12 and Stuttgart 20.2.12. Anthroposophic Press 1993.

Trauma versus karma

Modern reincarnation experience in the light of anthroposophy

Hans Peter van Manen

A century ago reincarnation was more or less an apocryphal concept. In the margin of the intellectual élite it had raised some interest even to the point of fascination. This interest was largely due to the theosophical movement. Theosophy was still a new phenomenon and had strong roots in the recent Hindu renaissance. From there concepts such as reincarnation and karma entered the European and American vocabulary. They had no place in the official culture, least of all in the new science of psychology. But in the course of this century the situation has thoroughly changed. In large parts of the world, more specifically in western culture, reincarnation has become a much discussed and popular concept. Experiences of different source and kind have given rise to a literature of its own. Anthroposophy has certainly, to a substantial degree, contributed to this growth of interest. In the last ten years especially the interest has expanded rapidly, strongly pushed by a new method of investigation: regression.

This method is often applied as a form of psychotherapy but it can also be practised for its own sake. It has clear affiliations with other psychotherapeutic methods that appeared earlier in the twentieth century, such as Sigmund Freud's psychoanalysis and the less known method of the *rêve éveillé,* the evoked dream (or guided fantasy). Regression can be applied in a purely individual way. Then the subject evokes his own experiences. But in most cases the psychotherapist or the leader of the session, sometimes with the assistance of others, guides the patient or the subject into the experience of a past life. Generally the subject is put in a lying position, often with eyes closed, like in a psychoanalytical session. Consciousness remains intact, although slightly dimmed. The session leader starts a dialogue with the subject and, without any haste, guides his attention to the past, youth, early childhood, infancy and then rather abruptly into spontaneous imaginations of what could be a former life. Then often the subject becomes active in describing vividly the situations of that life. Now and then the leader intervenes with a pointed question. The session can last an hour and a half, mostly not much more. The core of the method is to find the moment of crisis that can be seen as the cause of a main problem in the present life of the subject. Often a violent death or a violent shock of some kind appears as the traumatic experience, which, in its after effects, lingers on in the present life. The renewed conscious confrontation with the shocking experience brings relief to the patient and frees him from the oppression, at least according to the claims of the regressionists. So the Freudian concept of *trauma* is restored and widened into the field of previous incarnations.

A regressional session can be impressive. But immediately the question arises: how reliable are these experiences? Is there any guarantee that the imagined scenes are real reminiscences of a past life? Mostly the regressionists choose a pragmatic point of view to counter this question, saying that the value of the method is not constituted by the historical reality of the experience but by its healing effect. This pragmatic attitude which one finds also with Raymond Moody *(Life After Life,* 1989), may be understandable but leaves the most important question unanswered.

Connected with this question of the reliability is the problem of esoteric hygiene. On the difficult path towards initiation one can, without danger, enter the spirit world only when one 'crosses the threshold' with full consciousness. In a regression session one rather gets the impression that the subject, in a horizontal position, comfortably and unobviously passes under the threshold into – yes, into which world? The spirit world? Or the soul world? Or is it a transitional realm between our physical world and the soul world, a transitional sphere where reality and fantasy mix indiscriminately?

This uncertainty also remains in other kinds of current reincarnation experiences. About ten years ago the largely autobiographical books of Shirley Maclaine gained enormous popularity. One of the items she discussed and promoted in a New Age style was the method of 'channelling.' One could call it a neo-mediumistic approach to the supersensible. The practitioners are often compared with mediums, persons who with total exclusion of their own consciousness were supposed to serve as mouthpiece for the souls of deceased human beings. This practice has above all been cultivated since the middle of last century in spiritualistic circles. Now in the late twentieth century, the medium does not necessarily lose his complete consciousness but, just as in regression sessions, it is dimmed to a certain degree. He tries to serve as a channel for other beings. Sessions take place in the form of simple dialogues. After the session the medium mostly quickly forgets the details of the conversation. Sometimes in these sessions former lives are questioned. The problem of their possible reliability presents itself at least as strongly as with regression.

A revealing example of this questionable reliability is to be found in the partly autobiographical publication of Eugene Jussek *Conversations with Yan Su Lu* (German edition, 1986, preface by E. Kübler Ross). Jussek is a German who studied medicine and psychiatry and emigrated to California where he developed an interest in unusual healing methods. He describes at some length a case that absorbed his attention for a long time. A good-natured patient of very modest social and intellectual status suffers, without obvious reason, from spontaneous fits of gloom and aggression. Jussek subjects him to a combination of hypnosis, regression and channelling. In these sessions several supposed former lives of the patient come to the surface. Jussek's interest is focused on the last two of these. The patient himself is serving as channel but, after the sessions, he has no recollection of what has been revealed through his own mouth. The last but one 'life' was in early eighteenth century Ireland, in which he is supposed to have been an Irish rebel, persecuted, tortured and finally killed by the English oppressors. The second report speaks about an incarnation in England in the nineteenth century in Northampton. There he tells about an existence as a son of a well-to-do family. He inherited a leading position in a local bank, remained a bachelor, suffered frustrations, and had not made much of his life when he died at advanced middle age in 1861.

Jussek decides to go overseas to investigate possible traces of these human existences. In Ireland nothing can be found. The English had not kept registers of the rebels they liquidated. In Northampton circumstances are different. Despite some difficulties, the church and the churchyard provide recognizable evidence. Striking details confirm what the patient had revealed under hypnosis. In 1861 a person with a similar name (John instead of James Stewart) had been buried in a churchyard that fitted the description. But strangely enough other crucial details do not fit together at all. The person in question had been young when he died. His social status as an educated labourer had been very modest and he had certainly not been rich at all. For Jussek the corresponding details are decisive. The differences are of little consequence to him.

We relate this example because it is not very often that the reality of a reported life is investigated. One could at least ask whether this mixture of truth and wishful fantasy is perhaps present in many accounts of supposed former lives within or outside regression practices.

Another much discussed field of recent experiences is the growing number of young children's memories of possible former human lives (Ian Stevenson, *Twenty Cases Suggestive of*

Reincarnation, Charlottesville, 1974). These experiences are quite common, above all in India. In such cases a child stubbornly claims to have another name and to be at home in a village, which it can describe in detail, although it is beyond any doubt that the child, in his present existence, has ever been there. A number of these cases have been verified. Often it can be testified that the person with whom the child identifies itself had, indeed, lived and died in the village, mostly not very long ago. Often it is a person of the same sex but not always. The religion can be very different. Most of these accounts sprouted in the course of this century, but long before regression became fashionable. The same difficulty appeared here in this group of experiences. In one case a child caused surprise by the exactitude of its imagined observations but the person it described had only died some time *after* the present child's date of birth. There is, of course, much more evidence of this kind that underlines that the reality and the accuracy of the experiences present unsolved problems.

What light can anthroposophy shed on this field of experience? Anthroposophy is not a religious teaching. It claims to be a method of spiritual investigation and was worked out as such by Rudolf Steiner. It is often seen as a modification of old Hindu teachings in a theosophical framework. This is not the case. The first important aspect in which the anthroposophical version differs from other forms is that Steiner demonstrates how the concepts of reincarnation and karma constitute a logical consequence of the methods and the results of European scientific thinking. That, in general, the scientific world has not (yet) honoured this claim does not counter the fact that Steiner and other anthroposophists feel challenged by science and try to bring the two concepts into the orbit of human *knowledge (Reinkarnation und Karma vom Standpunkte der Naturwissenschaft notwendige Vorstellungen; Theosophy,* chapter 2).

The second main characteristic of Steiner's approach is that the priority lies with the concept of karma. This word indeed has been taken from Hinduism but, in the last instance, it can be viewed and experienced as a 'spiritual law of nature' as a most refined appearance of the law of cause and effect. In this view, karma and its laws have a nearly all-embracing importance not only at a philosophical level – where it can be seen as the complement of Steiner's 'philosophy of freedom' – but also at the practical levels of medicine and education. Now the centre of discipline of Steiner's anthroposophy is the esoteric inner schooling of the soul by which the soul refines itself gradually into an instrument of spiritual knowledge. The ability to tackle and recreate one's own karma can be seen as the most essential element of this way of schooling.

There is a third main difference between the European approach of anthroposophy and the Hinduistic–theosophical approach. Not only Hindu religion – and Buddhism – but also Hindu civilization in all its aspects is based on and permeated by the concept of karma. The framework is, curiously enough, strongly individualistic. The law of karma is a cosmic reality but it strictly applies to the conduct of the earthly human individual. Noble deeds and a pious attitude of life carry their fruit in improved outward life conditions in the next incarnation. Evil conduct is punished in the next incarnation by a lowering of caste and other probations. The prospect is serious but, to a certain extent, optimistic: in the end it is possible, in principle, to free the soul completely from all karmic burdens. But the background is a thoroughly pessimistic outlook on earthly life. Once free, the soul is discharged of the obligation to dive again and again through incarnations into the earthly world, where all evolution is but an illusion. The European concept, already present in the surprisingly original essay of G.E. Lessing on *The Education of the Human Genus* and later worked out by Steiner in a whole range of publications, widens the concept. *Menschheitskarma,* the destiny of mankind; this wording indicates that humanity, as such, is moving towards an aim in a distant future. The karma of the human individual is sublimated by those actions that contribute to the future of mankind and, accordingly, complicates itself by deviations from this course. In this process Christ appears as the coordinator of cosmic justice, as Lord of karma.

A fourth characteristic must be mentioned: the law of *metamorphosis,* which intertwines with the law of karma. It implies different aspects. For instance, the circumstances of one incarnation do not purely repeat themselves in a next life. Indeed, in many novels that deal with reincarnation – such as the one-time popular novels by Joan Grant – the scenes and circumstances change only at the surface; the relations, and often the emotions too, remain unchanged. In the anthroposophical view the reality of karma is very different. The new circumstances often show completely reversed roles, deep changes of character and mostly a shift of talents. The examples that Steiner gave in his famous karma lectures in 1924 – one year before his death – are not meant in a dogmatic way but just as examples to show, first, how vivid and deep such changes can be and, second, to demonstrate with how much consequence the development of the human individual rules over these changes.

Here lies one of the great points of difference between, on one side, many modern accounts, especially but not only, collected through regression, and the anthroposophical view. To say it clearly: just as in the above-mentioned fiction, the element of metamorphosis is absent in most of these cases. And in combination with that another difference becomes manifest. According to Steiner, time between two incarnations encompasses as a rule several centuries, whereas in regression and other contemporary accounts generally the intervals are not longer than a few decades.

These indications confront us with a separate difficulty that can be solved rather easily. Originally Steiner spoke about once in two thousand years, but he meant once as a man and once as a woman, so twice in total. On the other hand, one must take into account that there are many exceptions to this rule. When a child dies it normally reincarnates very soon. Accordingly, people who die at a young age return within decades. So the *average* interval between two earthly existences is much less than the 'normal' interval. As a consequence of this, one can conclude that the thorough change along the lines of metamorphosis manifests much less strongly in a complementing incarnation soon after the last interrupted one than usual, which means after a long interval between death and rebirth. Now, in most current accounts, the time between the supposed incarnations is short. This could, of course, mean that traumatic experiences have not yet been digested and transformed and, after the quick return, still show their after effects.

Yet there is reason for serious doubt, whether these accounts in general are genuine. Experiences of violence such as murder or torture can indeed be so strong that after death they do not dissolve lightly. This requires a short explanation. In the anthroposophical view man does not consist only of soul and body but a soul is enshrined in the three envelopes of physical, etheric and astral body. The etheric outlives the physical body after death only for a few days and dissolves then in the etheric cosmos. The astral body lingers on for quite a time. 'Astral body' means the complex unity of the emotions, inclinations, talents of an incarnated person. It only gradually dissolves when, after the physical death, the soul digests and objectivates the part-earthly life. This implies that certain very heavy emotional experiences linger on in the astral world as stubbornly insoluble ingredients. Such ingredients eventually can present themselves to other people, who longingly reach back to their 'former life' and subsequently slip into these 'astral vestments,' laid off by other souls.

When we try and make up the balance of our considerations so far, we may with caution conclude that a good deal of the modern accounts of previous incarnations may be authentic, although they do not constitute the rule, and that many may be illusory. This cautious and inexact estimate still circumvents the most delicate problem. That problem is the fact that this whole flood of experiences, and especially the findings of regression, obscure the reality of karma. To put it in a more pointed way: in regression the concept of trauma is put in the place of karma.

So far we have treated revelations from regression sessions and spontaneous reminiscences more or less as events of the same kind. This is not quite justified. For, in some cases, this spontaneous memory has a stronger claim to be taken seriously. We take as a first example the case described in detail by Arthur Guirdham in *The Cathars and Reincarnation* (1970). It became known years before the wave of regression came up. The author, a physician, had among his patients a woman who was haunted by impressions from medieval southern France, in which she felt she had been involved in the life-and-death struggle of the most powerful heresy of Catharism. Her most urgent wish is to be freed from these impressions. At first Guirdham concludes that basically she is a stable, healthy person. He then starts to investigate her claims through study and travelling and finds historic details that never could have been assembled by the patient herself. An extra reason for his interest is caused by the fact that his patient recognizes in him the man whom she followed and loved in that time. The dramatic culmination of these memories is the death at the stake of both of them (together with others). This experience is described in so much detail that one indeed comes to the impression that here a trauma was engraved so deeply in the astral body that it had to be lived through again in a new earthly existence to be got rid of and to be dissolved. Before having had any encounter with regression methods, I had qualified the experience of Guirdham's patient as a 'trauma' in the sense given above. To be quite clear: here, as in many other cases, one is not in the realm of certainty but still at a higher level than the level of mere possibility. One moves along the path of probability.

The many cases of younger people living with the intuitive 'knowledge' that they lived and died young in World War II, many of them in connection with the holocaust can be considered as a category of its own. Often these recollections are inarticulate, just in the form of an inward certainty. Of particular interest are two publications. One is the report of a Jewish rabbi on the interviews he had with a number of these younger people. The other example is Barbro Karlen. She is a young woman in Sweden who became famous for two reasons. As a teenager she caused surprise by her literary talent. Her first volume of poetry became a bestseller. The second reason was that she discovered in herself clear pictures with the quality of remembered scenes of the life of Anne Frank. She did not try to convince public opinion but she felt it as a certainty within herself, at first spoke freely about it and soon became very cautious. After a time she avoided any further discussion. Again, the question presents itself: how can one ever be certain of the authenticity of such communications? Scientific knowledge requires certainty and not probability. The answer can be that here we have to do with probabilities that sooner or later can develop into clear certainties. It can, for instance, happen through spontaneously converging experiences of different people. To give an example based on repeated experience, I have formed the impression that a living person whom I know could have been a certain well-known personality of the past. It is important that one is able to remain silent about it so that the impression can either wither or ripen. Withering means in this case that the idea gradually fades away; ripening, the idea gains stability, which is not yet the same as certainty. Then karma can intervene in the following way. The person in question has died, one meets a friend who was at his death bed and who knew nothing of my impression of the deceased person's previous life. Then all of a sudden, by a flash of inspiration, he arrives at the same impression: that the deceased person was identical with the historic individual I had in mind. Then one has moved into the orbit of certainty. Whether one should speak or even write about it is a completely different question.

From the side of regression practitioners, an often heard counter-criticism to objections like the ones made in this article is that anthroposophists dogmatically turn Steiner into an absolute criterion. This may be so in some cases but, in its essence, this is a misunderstanding. Steiner showed different ways through which the student himself can come to a knowing experience of reincarnation. In the books mentioned from the beginning of the century he very clearly outlines how, by a consistent process of observation and thinking, one can arrive at a conclusion that karma is a reality. We will not elaborate on that. One must by one's own study develop this experience. It is not an outwardly convincing proof based on scientific evidence. But people forget that the reality of an inward or outward fact can never be proved. Proof always moves in the realm of hypothesis. The reality of a fact can only be experienced. Such an experience can only rest on an act of freedom. A cohesive range of thoughts such as Steiner's presentation of the concept of karma can evoke such an experience. It is characterized by a complete clarity, free from any mysticism.

This logical approach is not theoretical at all but can make a very theoretical impression. However, Steiner indicates another very practical method of coming to grips with one's own karma. He gives a variety of different so-called karma exercises, most of which all share the aim of trying to identify oneself with all the adverse aspects that occur in one's path of life, for instance, frustrations in one's career or purely accidental injuries. In the year 1912 he suggested building up a picture of a person who embodies all the negative experiences with which one is confronted. This shadowy counter-personality soon loses its ghostlike quality; it starts to become familiar. And, after a short while, one recognizes it as one's own deeper self. This may not sound convincing when one reads it. But here, too, the proof can only lie in the experience as it evolves from the exercise. The final effect is not that one 'sees' one's previous incarnation; the most important result is the strengthened resolve to meet the limitations in one's present life creatively.

Angels amongst us

Hartwig Schiller

> Let us look upon ourselves as human beings whom karma has brought to this place where something is to happen which shall surpass ordinary events – something which may make all participants here feel that they have witnessed a festive moment of world destiny.[1]

These words were spoken by Rudolf Steiner on 21 August 1919 when he began the training of teachers during the founding of the first Waldorf School in Stuttgart. This affirmation of the significance of karma in the pedagogical impulse followed immediately after the esoteric opening of the first lecture in the cycle now known as *The Study of Man*. This opening was for many years known only to a few, but is now published.[2]

It is not only the moment he chose for these words that seems remarkable, their content and formulation are also striking. Those present are told that the work they are now embarking upon is not the result of a spontaneous or coincidental decision. On the contrary, karma placed *each one of us* in our position at this historic moment. Yet we do not come to it alone. We are part of a group: let *us* look upon *ourselves*. At the end this is described as the experience of a *festive moment of world history*. Thus he places it in the context of time. Time, however, extends beyond any one individual or group. Time has an epoch-making effect for humanity as a whole.

The importance of karma in relation to the founding of the school is thus highlighted at three levels: the individual, the relationship of the group and the epoch-making effect. Thus attention is drawn to a variety of karmic perspectives relating to the school. Before we look at each one in detail, we should try to clarify the concept of karma. As a basis for this, we can take the first lecture in the cycle, *Manifestations of Karma,* given on 16 May 1910 in Hamburg.[3] This lecture begins in a way that is most unusual for Steiner. He begins a cycle of eleven lectures with a definition — the definition of karma. His subsequent remarks make it clear that it is more of a characterization or descriptive approach than an abstract definition.

Rudolf Steiner sets out five fundamental aspects of karma:

- to begin with two beings have an encounter that leads to a developing relationship, the one has an effect on the other;
- within this relationship each participant experiences the consequences of his own actions;
- the consequences of the resultant relationship are not fully perceived at the time;
- karma fulfils itself as a process, there is a period of time between cause and effect;
- the whole process has an inherent lawfulness that extends beyond the momentary awareness of those affected, the lawful consequences are not consciously determined by the beings concerned.

Some of these truths are beautifully reflected in fairy tales. Grimm's *Mother Holle* describes the adventures of a girl who responds to the situations she finds herself in out of her generosity of heart and selfless good nature, for which in the end she is richly rewarded with gold. When her envious step-sister then contrives to replicate the same situations out of avarice she is rewarded with pitch.

Karmic connections may only be approached in a chaste and selfless way. They are not accessible to calculating reason. They contain a greater wisdom than that of any human being. If it were not so, karma would have no meaning – it would simply continue the errors and entanglements of life without bringing to bear its harmonizing and healing effect.

The forces that shape karma

What forces are at work in shaping karma? We can pursue this question with some precision in the specific context of the words quoted from the founding of the school. They were spoken by Rudolf Steiner after he had conducted a kind of opening ceremony that he described as, '... a kind of prayer addressed to those powers who, working through Imaginations, Inspirations and Intuitions, are to stand behind us as we take on this task.'[4]

We have been given quite precise details of this 'prayer' in the notes of three of those present: Caroline von Heydebrand, Herbert Hahn and Walter Johannes Stein. These may now be studied in the appendix to the recent publication of *Study of Man.*[5]

The entry in W.J. Stein's diary is pithy:

Beginning of the course. Opened by Dr Steiner, 9.00.
    Strength – Angels
    Courage – Archangels
    Light – Archai
[He] thanks the ... (good spirits), who gave Molt the idea. The gods will work on with the consequences of our deeds.

If this was all we had to go on we would probably have greater difficulty in understanding what went on. We would, perhaps, know that the beings of the third hierarchy were the content of the 'prayer,' and that the qualities of strength, courage and light had been related to them. We would, however, not know how the third hierarchy is connected with the founding of the school, nor would we know its significance for the karmic meeting of those present.

It is the notes made by Caroline von Heydebrand and Herbert

Hahn that will help us here. The most comprehensive and detailed report is Caroline von Heydebrand's, written shortly before her death in 1938. Its contents are in exact accord with the earlier and rather shorter diary entry of Herbert Hahn, which is undated. Hahn wrote a more extensive version in 1967, which is now perhaps the most widely known. It also covers broadly the same ground as the other versions.[6] We shall now take a closer look at Caroline von Heydebrand's version. According to this, Rudolf Steiner spoke of the following sequence of events.

> We wish to form our thoughts in such a way that we may be conscious that:
> Behind every one of us stands his Angel, gently laying his hands on our heads. This Angel gives you the strength you need.
> Above your heads there hover the circling Archangels. They carry from one to the other what each has to give. They unite your souls. Thereby you are given the courage of which you stand in need. (Out of this courage the Archangels form a chalice.)
> The light of wisdom is given to us by the exalted beings of the Archai, who are not limited to the circling movements, but who, coming forth from primal beginnings, manifest themselves and disappear into primal distances. They reveal themselves only in form of drop (of light) in this place. (Into the chalice of courage there falls a drop of light, enlightening our times, bestowed by the ruling Spirit of our Age.)

After the closure of the Stuttgart school, Caroline von Heydebrand told her Dutch friends about this event. Then she gave them, as she did a little later to her English friends, a copy to preserve some memory of these events. These recollections are as helpful now as they were then in linking us with the foundation of the Waldorf School, and enabling us to recognize the powers it bears for the future.

Within this description we can recognize the three levels on which those present were brought together by karma as indicated in the opening quotation from Rudolf Steiner.

Thus the working of the third hierarchy as a whole becomes clear. The Angel has to do with the spirituality of the individual human being, with his own self. The Archangel works in connection with groups of people. That generally involves working in a spatial dimension, for groups of human beings are generally geographically close to one another in a shared space. Spirits of Time on the other hand work in a particular epoch, affecting the whole of humanity. The situation of the individual in space and time is made visible in the working of the third hierarchy.

The guiding role of the third hierarchy before birth

The human being is deeply connected with the beings of the third hierarchy in all that concerns his individual development. They are of particular help to him in the transition from his prebirth state into earthly life. In the small child we can still sense that this is a matter of direct experience. The child encounters the world with a remarkable power of devotion. If one wished to characterize this devotion more precisely, one could describe the child's attitude as one of blissful confidence. More commonly, we speak of the child's power of imitation. The full importance of this becomes clear, however, when we realize that in this phase of child development the fundamental capacities of the human being unfold. After all, it is imitation that leads the child to the activities of walking, speaking and thinking. Yet the child does not seem particularly choosy in this phase.

The manner in which one walks and speaks, the depth or superficiality of one's thinking, all have their effect on the child. It can be quite shocking for parents to see how particular expressions or patterns of behaviour reappear in their children. Thus the child might incline its head in a particular way while listening, or it might be unduly verbose, or again suddenly interrupt the speaker. One way or the other, parents will see themselves reflected in their children.

Thus the imitated environment of the child truly becomes its destiny. Such is the strength of the child's power of trust. It is total devotion, unquestioned, unchecked, uncritical.

This quality of devotion has its roots in the prebirth experiences of the child. The child is not yet weaned from the spiritual world to the extent that the adult is. That world is, after all, not so remote.

The baby remains close to the spiritual world in the long periods of sleep it has after birth. Moreover the sleep of a little child still has a different quality to that of an adult. It does not have anything like the amount of daytime experiences to digest, and so sleep is not so strong a contrast to the daytime experience as is the case with the adult. Before its birth, the child had experienced the work of spiritual beings preparing with him for earthly life. The beings of the third hierarchy were particularly helpful to it in learning to walk, speak and think. Rudolf Steiner describes how, on the way to birth, the Angels help prepare the development for thinking after birth, the Archangels the development of speech, and the Archai the development of walking.[7] Moreover, this happens in the symmetrical sequence implied. The Angels stand at the beginning and at the end of this development. Before birth, the Archangels follow the Angels with their work, and after birth they precede them. The same applies to the Archai. The Archai live in the element of will, which is connected with walking, the Archangels introduce into speech the inner gesture of the feeling life with its flowing to and fro from the one to the other, and the Angels form the development of thinking, which can survey all before it. It is because the human being follows these spiritual beings with an attitude of devotion before it is born that this attitude works on so strongly after birth. This is why the child is an imitative being in the first seven years of its life.

Higher learning

There is naturally a great difference between the activities of walking, speaking and thinking before birth, and what the human being does in this way after birth. Rudolf Steiner describes how in the course of evolution humanity has learned to think under the guidance of the Angels,[8] but then goes on to contrast the angelic and human thinking. We think by laboriously going from point to point in a process that takes time, Angels have an instinctive life of thought in which an entire thought construction appears instantly as a reflective consciousness.

It becomes clear how much greater and more powerful the activity of thinking is in the Angel. They can see the situation in its entirety, immediately and in perspective. And now, perhaps, it can also become clear why Rudolf Steiner describes the Angels in a particular attitude, and having a particular activity in the esoteric ceremony at the beginning of *Study of Man*.

> Behind each of us stands his Angel, gently laying his hands on the head of each – this Angel gives you the strength you need.

This quality of spiritual consciousness, the thinking of the Angels, has its contents in the form of comprehensive pictures, or Imaginations. Rudolf Steiner was referring to these when he spoke of this ceremony as:

> a kind of prayer addressed to those powers who, working through Imaginations, Inspirations and Intuitions, are to stand behind us as we take on this task.

It is the Angels who can awaken the power of Imagination in the human soul. By the same token, the Archangels' teaching of speaking should not be thought of in terms of human speech, conversation or the exchange of words. With the Archangels, speech means a revelation of being that is communicated to the other being as an experience. A revelation of being means that one being communicates itself to the other so that it completely fills the other. It occupies the space of the other being. For this to take place the other being has to prepare itself. This preparing involves the creating of space, the emptying of consciousness. This may seem paradoxical, because in such circumstances ordinary human consciousness is lost. However, the communication of being can only take place in such circumstances. The process always involves the quality of courage, for what has been described in the conversation of the Archangels requires the renunciation of all that has been attained hitherto. It is a making oneself ready for something completely new, other and unexpected. It is a matter of placing oneself at another's disposal. In this way, what is spoken of as the 'prayer' can come about: 'they unite your souls' as 'they carry from one to the other what each has to give to the other.' This activity is an Inspiring of those present.

A third step is involved when we look at how the Archai teach us to walk. The human earthly activity of walking is only an outer image of their spiritual activity. The Archai give impulses – their being is Initiative. Just as the human being lives somewhat unconsciously in his will when he walks, so the beings of the Archai live in a purely spiritual element of will. Also, for human beings, any deed of will relies on a union of the doer and the deed, of exercising the will and changing the world. In the case of the Archai, this union is a conscious, forming creation of being. Their deeds communicate being and give impulse to being. From their region a community of human beings can receive an experience of the purpose and potential of their own activity: 'the light of wisdom is given to us by the exalted beings of the Archai.' The necessary Intuitions come to those working in the community from the region of light.

The school community

This then gives us exact and practical indications on how to deal with the question of karmic relationships in a school community: karma becomes three dimensional. First there is the dimension of the individual human being in the care of his Angel as he progresses from incarnation to incarnation. The Angel preserves in him earthly lives, and has become individual substance. Thus is developed the first of those members of the human being that are, as yet, only present in him in seed form: the Spirit Self.[9] His own development gives the individual human being a certain power that he can let stream into his work. He can bring strength to his work.

It is not, however, merely a matter of demonstrating or exercising this strength. Rather it is apparent in the work of the community as it streams from one to the other. This is a whole new quality. Strength is drawn into a weaving activity. What passes from the one to the other is woven into something that is shared. Thus something higher can come about which must be carried by a higher form of consciousness, the consciousness of a spirit of community, an Archangelic being. The human beings involved create the conditions for this to come about. The individual releases the fruit of his spiritual striving, and places it at the disposal of the others: in doing so, he releases into the community his most intimate possession, his spiritual child, entrusting it to the goodwill of the others – for he cannot know or predict what will come of it. He brings the fruits of his striving as a gift. As a true gift it comes with no strings attached, no demands, no intentions and no claims. The revelation of being is always without reserve. In this way, the gift acquires the quality of a sacrifice. The giver renounces all control over what is done with his contribution. It is not his will but that of the community. Anyone who devotes himself in this way to a group of people or to a situation needs courage, indeed is exercising courage. Letting go requires active courage. Nevertheless, positive examples given without ambition have an encouraging effect on others. In this connection courage is both active and passive. Courage arises between people — it is a phenomenon of relationships. Thus the germ is born of the substance that will appear in the future as Life Spirit. Today it still belongs to the nature of Archangelic beings.

It is critical for a community whether it serves its own purposes, or sets out to be the instrument of a higher purpose. In the former case, it sets itself apart from the whole and becomes a clique or an interest group. In the latter case, it develops a selfless quality, fulfilling itself as it fulfils its task. Therein lies the difference between a mere grouping and a community. It depends on the quality of what unites people, and what type of tasks a community can undertake and fulfil. In such a community, everything depends on the setting of the aims. In this sense, it has something of the quality of light. It is light that opens one's eyes, revealing things in their true relationships and conditions. Without light, all action in the world is a blind prodding and probing. With the founding of the Waldorf school, the intention is to allow the light of the Spirit of the Age to be present in the vessel of the community. This will make it possible to take up the tasks of humanity in our time — to meet the pressing need of our time in the light of the Spirit of the Age is the highest aim and task of all concerned. Only at this stage of development does the activity of human beings acquire sovereignty. Thus is revealed a first indication of that future member of the human being, Spirit Man, which has the nature of the Archai.

The strength of the individual

Against this background we can trace the karmic aspects of working together in the school community much more concretely.

There is, to begin with, the individual. What he can do for the common cause, how he can take part, all this depends initially on his personal capacities, his gifts. He acts out of the strength of his personality. He does, indeed, bring all that he has become, the totality of his past, to bear. Naturally, he will set out with all kinds of intentions from his prebirthly state. He will have set himself new tasks and aims. Nevertheless, he is a temporal being in a process of development and, like everything in being, he bears within him that which has not yet been transformed.

In his work with others, he will surprise them with all kinds of idiosyncrasies. Above all, he will surprise himself. In many ways others will find it easier to see him as he is than he will himself. They experience how he is in certain situations. What then happens they will frequently describe as typical. They seem to expect certain things of him, yet when they are asked why, it is not always so easy to explain. Such things are often completely incomprehensible to the person concerned. 'Why does this always happen to me?' is often asked.

To find out what truly belongs to one's own person requires a process of thoroughgoing self-knowledge. There are certain conditions to this. It must be honest, clear, consequent, fearless, conscientious and impartial. Humour is a great asset. The study of one's own personality should exert no greater fascination than a preoccupation with a weather report from a distant continent. The investigator should look at himself 'from above' and carry out certain experiments. One of the experiments Rudolf Steiner recommended is to take the view that one placed oneself in those very situations which at first seem incomprehensible, surprising and unpleasant. One's first reaction might be that one would never voluntarily place oneself in such a situation. Nevertheless, the experiment should be carried out deliberately, and with an attitude of 'wait and see.' Then, after a while, one should carefully observe whether or not a particular impression is gained. One eventually acquires the feeling that it is just these undesirable situations that are ideally suited to bring about the very development that an intimate self-knowledge would say one most needed. One thus appears to oneself as an unexpected opponent. Anyone who carries out such a process of self-observation will soon be very much better informed as to what contribution he can make to the community, or how best he can put his strength to use.

The courage for community

On the second level of karmic relationship, things look different. We had noted that, on this level, we are dealing with groups of people or geographical connections. They might be a class of pupils, a College of Teachers, a parent body, a particular school community, but also the local community in which a school is situated, a country or even a language grouping. Today, in the age of individualism, many people believe they are not influenced by such connections. Nevertheless, anyone who has lived in a foreign country and has experienced what a formative force is exerted by the mother tongue or the culture of a locality will know just how strong an influence they can exert. It is remarkable that this can be found even in quite small groups. Thus even Waldorf Schools in the same country can have quite strong differing regional characteristics. Even in cities where there are several schools one can observe distinct peculiarities in the corporate culture of each school.

The karmic meaning of such groups is best observed when you can work regularly with a particular group. A College of Teachers provides ample opportunity for observation of this kind. Much can be gained from observing polarities at work. Who, for example, is a given person's 'karmic opponent'? Or who always takes the opposite point of view? For the group as a whole, both people are essential – only when they are together do they actually make sense. Who is the slowest, who is the fastest? Who is progressive, who is conservative? Who is Prometheus, who is Epimetheus?

Oddly enough, almost every community will contain people who were born in a different region. Often they refer to their chosen country with a certain ironic detachment. So what leads them to these groups? It is difficult today to argue that they were brought there by outer necessity; rather, in the sense of the previous exercise, they will be there for reasons of their own choosing. One has to discover these reasons in an affirmative spirit. The alternative is to tilt at windmills like a latter-day Don Quixote. It is all the more difficult for a community if there is also a Sancho Panza to accompany the blind man on his self-appointed crusade.

Karma always requires an attitude of affirmation. We have to be able to say, 'Yes' to our own reality. The reality of a group can generally be experienced in its abundance of contradictory and complementary elements. Generally one has just such a role to play oneself.

The spirit of the age

In his address given the evening before he began the lecture cycle *Study of Man,* Rudolf Steiner concluded with the words:

> We can only draw from what can be gained today by directing our interest firstly to the great need of our time, and secondly, to the great tasks of our time, both of which are greater than we can imagine.[10]

This is an example of an affirmative attitude to karma on the level of the age we live in. The human being is born into a particular epoch. Every epoch involves change and upheaval, yet some epochs have this characteristic more than others. Our time certainly shows no lack of tumultuous change. There are countless complaints in pedagogical discussions about the demands made on teachers today. People generally point to the dissolution of social ties, the annual increase in the divorce rate, the increasing number of only children. The decay of social mores and norms are also part of this picture. Alongside this, one deplores the loss of values, guidelines or a given sense of purpose. People often see a connection with the role of the media in our society. Even a normally developing human soul is scarcely capable of dealing with the deluge of pictures, sounds and experiences to which the adolescent is exposed daily. One can point to a loss of communion with nature, and to the prevalent alienation of the human being. Many teachers have observed that this can only lead to the dissolution of the individual ego, and with it the dignity of man.

Are these teachers so entirely wrong? Surely not. But does such a view of the dramatic aberrations, perils and abysses of the present do justice to the whole picture of our age. Equally surely not! Or would a more human alternative be an idyll of harmonious bliss in traditional order and secure social forms? It is only too easy to take leave of the tempests of our epoch and wish for the calmer waters of more comfortable circumstances.

One is, however, a child of one's time. It is no coincidence that we have been born into this time. On the contrary, it is our prebirth intentions that have placed us where we are! All the furious pace of change, the overturning of old norms and traditions and the challenges these pose, were quite clear from that perspective. What was wanted was the dawn of a new, spiritual foundation for life! This is, however, only possible if the old traditional ways and norms are dissolved. These are the hallmarks of a Michaelic Age that bears with it storms, disasters and struggles. For only the downfall of the old can bring about the rise of what lies innermost in the soul. Presence of mind as a human attribute lives in a dynamic of its own creation. Only in affirming the great need of our time will one be able to find the spiritual sources and remedies with which to meet it. Dire need and human dignity are two sides of the same coin. Among many other things it belongs to the Michaelic Age in which we live that each of us take up his cross, and with it the certainty that no one is given more than he can bear. For Michael is the countenance of Christ. Thus the threefold karmic perspective that appears at the beginning of the school foundation is the affirmation of the strength of the individual, the gaze into the mirror of the community and the taking up of the tasks that face us in the age in which we live. On this basis, each of us can develop a concrete impression of what is the karma of the individual, the community and the age.

Pedagogical practice

When the teacher becomes concerned with questions of karma the first feeling he is likely to have when confronted with a child is, 'You are not a blank sheet of paper.' 'Something is living in you which is seeking its further development from a prebirthly state through the experiences of a new earthly life.'

The question he may well then ask himself is, 'How can I help the child in this endeavour?' In order to do this one needs to know something about the child, something about its inner being. This pedagogical attitude is an achievement of the twentieth century. This is quite generally the case even with certain individual teachers from whom one would least expect it. It is very directly evident in the motto of the so-called progressive teachers: start with the child! This motto means, after all, that it is not the educational whims of the adults that are to be imposed on the children, but rather that the child itself is the measure of what is required.

Rudolf Steiner also affirmed this attitude in the progressive movement in his essay, *Free Education and the Threefold Social Order*, in which he demands that no aspect of social order, political or economic intentions should exert an influence on the child during its education. Only the individual predispositions of the child and the general laws of development (which always involve some degree of social adjustment) should determine the way in which education is carried out.[11] Such considerations are prevalent in the way teaching has developed today. Yet even though there may well be a consensus on this today, one problem remains to be solved, namely the question, 'Who are you?.'

To answer this question, the educator today has to learn to read karma. The book of humanity lies open before him, the symbols are written in the child, its surroundings, life circumstances, friends, enemies and the times in which it lives. But the educator must notice them, must put the letters together, must learn to read, must see and understand connections. In the moment of encounter, he must recognize the influence of the past, and the striving towards the future. He must, at the very least, awaken in himself a kind of new instinct, a kind of divining receptivity for this task.

He will be helped in this if he undertakes exercises of the kind referred to above in respect of his own karmic disposition. Once more, it is a matter of taking a dispassionate interest in the totality of the life circumstances and impulses of the individual human being. To direct one's teaching on the basis of the requirements of the child, one has first of all to get to know the child. The first indications that can provide a guideline in this will be gathered from the harvest of loving and careful observations.

The next step involves the creation of a picture of the child that makes sense. This picture should come about quite independently of personal inclinations, sympathy or antipathy, even of pedagogical intentions. As in any picture which, despite all appearances, can only exist in two dimensions, one detail stands beside another. Nothing is obscured, nothing is permitted to conceal anything else. The evaluation of what is there is based on the relationship of one detail to another, and on the impression given by the whole. This inner consonance, which allows one to discover the composition of the picture, enables us to understand it. Having once worked in such a way, one will always find that one's personal relationship to the child undergoes a change immediately afterwards. If the study has been carried out in the scrupulous way indicated, the relationship will be closer and more intimate.

What is not at issue here is to find out 'who' the child may have been in a previous life, and 'where' and 'how.' Appropriate efforts and a selfless devotion to exercises will always be able to reveal further details of this type, but sensation mongering and curiosity will render all such efforts fruitless. All such 'interests' are quite irrelevant, if not superfluous, to the pedagogical task. Karma research requires a chaste attitude, and the work of the educator is directed towards shaping the future of the human being. Whatever is fruitful for that will reveal itself in the course of study.

From space to time

It would be a mistake to believe that the work described above in forming a picture of the child's individuality is the end of the story. Rather it is only a first stage. This picture, however carefully made, will only contain a part of the truth. It is necessary to complete this picture by setting it against the pictures made by others. That is the purpose of the child study in the Teachers' Meeting. The one shares with the other his impressions of the child. In this way, those present open each other's eyes and, in doing so, each of them enriches, changes and develops his view of the child. Enriched by the views of others, the picture comes back to its initiator, who has now modified his view through those of the others, and only now is in a position to accompany the child's development with a true understanding.

From time to time one hears from Colleges what a remarkable effect such child studies have. They report significant effects. Successful child studies do not seek for quick results or immediate strategies. They provide space for ideas. Such ideas may take time to reveal themselves. Often they come overnight or some time later. Attentive colleagues will suddenly notice that a real change has taken place in the development of the child, and on looking back can see the connection.

The child study in the College of Teachers has become an instrument. The College has formed something like a vessel into which an idea that will further the child's development can be poured. This process involves no self-deluding mysticism. It comes about through clear and conscious practice. Those who take part can see and understand what is going on with their thinking. The more unambiguous, exact and thorough the observations that have flowed into the child study, the more productive will be the results.

A community with spiritual foundations

The experiences referred to above in the area of education show how fruitful it can be to take account of karma and of the beings of the third hierarchy. These things can also be applied to the whole school community and other social connections, for they contain the fundamentals of all social forms that have spiritual foundations. This is true on three levels.

We start with the individual. He would like to be accepted into the circle of those who are working together. He has to be allowed the possibility of taking initiative and carrying responsibility. He must be able to take his work seriously and to do it without constantly being questioned by supervision, censure or reservations. Naturally there are common goals that have brought people together in the first place. But these goals do not have a guarantee of validity for all eternity. They must be continually reaffirmed at all three levels.

The second level is that of co-operation. The individual is dependent on being able to exchange with the other members of the community. Where it is not possible to develop a common consciousness, where there is no meeting of the community as a whole, there is no possibility of experiencing the second level. This is one of the realities of community building. It also depends on the tasks involved, on the people involved and on the appropriate ways of working. To have an experience of a language grouping, it is not necessary to meet all its members and be in regular touch with them. For a College of Teachers, however, this experience is essential. Where common tasks are exclusively delegated to committees, where there is no common study, and those concerned only meet each other in passing, there cannot be the stimulating and correcting influence of the others. The forming of a chalice can only be achieved when people work together directly, or the shards will consider themselves chalices. Cliques always believe that they alone have found what really matters.

In fact, what really matters can only be found in the totality.

This is a phenomenon of the third level. To make visible what really matters requires that every individual contributes in a specific and unique way. At this level, the value of the individual loses itself in the whole, for without the individual the totality could not be formed. From a spiritual point of view, community forming depends on unity. Unity in plurality — that is the principle of modern contemporary community forming. It can only come about in a dynamic process in which the three layers are always addressed simultaneously and in different ways. One person will gain strength for his work from clear aims and tasks. With another it is his strength that brings him to eventual clarity. A third will find strength and clarity in the experience of team work and comradeship.

A contemporary approach to karma

A community that wishes to take karma into account must work in this way. The human being is an integrated being, living as an individual in space and time. From his previous earthly lives he has created the circumstances and tasks of his present life. Positive community building, which seeks to help achieve karmic challenges, must be based on affirmation, acceptance of the other and of one's own humanity, both of which always belong to us. For that is the meaning of karma: my surroundings belong to me. I am my surroundings. The fulfilment of karma, and one's tasks, means the acceptance of one's fellow human beings, means recompense, reconciliation and healing. Thus the five aspects of karma referred to at the beginning come to fulfilment:

- human beings meet and have an effect on each other;
- this has its consequence for each individual;
- this is not at first apparent;
- time passes between cause and effect;
- the after-effects are other than what was expected.

Practical work on the karma of the individual by groups of people, or for the time in which we find ourselves, can only be carried out in a healthy way if it is done in the spirit of humility, faithfulness and integrity. Working on karma in the context of present day western civilization amounts to practical Christianity.

References

1. Steiner, Rudolf, *Study of Man.* GA 293. What is referred to here (see also notes 2, 4 and 5 below) appears only in the latest German edition: *Allgemeine Menschenkunde,* Rudolf Steiner Verlag, Dornach 1992.
2. Ibid.
3. Steiner, Rudolf, *The Manifestations of Karma,* Rudolf Steiner Press, 1984.
4. Steiner, Rudolf, *Study of Man.*
5. Ibid.
6. Hann's reference in 1967 to the 'Teaching Staff' is not found in the early notes of Stein, Heydebrand and Hahn. The latter refer to all those present, including Emil and Berta Molt as school sponsors and parents, as well as other anthroposophists who had been invited for the occasion. This is clear from Heydebrand's text referred to above.
7. Steiner, Rudolf, *Man's Being, His Destiny and World Evolution,* GA 226, Lecture of 18 May 1923. Anthroposophic Press, New York 1966.
8. Steiner, Rudolf, *The Spiritual Guidance of Humanity,* Anthroposophic Press, New York 1970.
9. The terms 'Spirit Self,' 'Life Spirit' and 'Spirit Man' were used by Rudolf Steiner to designate future stages of human evolution. These are described more fully in his book *Theosophy,* Rudolf Steiner Press, London 1973.
10. The version reproduced here is based on the incomplete notes made by Rudolf Meyer and those made by Emil Molt and Karl Stockmeyer. The text was by Erich Gabert. It may be found in the 1992 edition of *Study of Man* and some earlier editions.
11. Steiner, Rudolf, "Aufsatze über die Dreigliederung des sozialen Organismus und zur Zeitlage," 1915–1921, Dornach 1982, GA 24. *The Renewal of the Social Organism,* Anthroposophic Press, 1985.

Karma and the Internet

Dorit Winter

> Our era has seen an escalation of the rate of change so drastic that all possibilities of evolutionary accommodation have been short-circuited ... We have created the technology that not only enables us to change our basic nature, but that is making such change all but inevitable.[1]

Perhaps it is not intemperate to suggest that both the rate of change and the inevitability of the change to our basic nature may be measured by the upsurge of Internet use by anthroposophists. To wit: the next *Directory of the Anthroposophical Society* in North America will include e-mail addresses; the Goetheanum has a home page on the Internet; Waldorf teachers in California are in on-line dialogue with counterparts in Brazil.[2]

Constantly striving to be accepted as legitimate by the culture that surrounds us, we are already part of it. The computer culture permeates our habit lives just as necessarily as substances in the air permeate our physical organs. Consciousness about food, water, air, warmth and the rest of our physical needs is established within the general culture under the rubric 'health food,' thus allowing anthroposophists to purchase organic (if not biodynamic) foods in non-anthroposophical shops; and the threefold nature of the human being has been generally recognized (if not clearly understood) so that soul and spirit are acceptable terms in the relatively well-established realms of alternative medicine and even alternative education. However, the fourfold nature of the human being is a more occult reality, and the etheric body still a largely hidden concept. So whereas the culture that surrounds us, and of which we are part, contains small, perhaps tenuous, but nevertheless viable 'alternative' parklands, which may even include anthroposophical preserves, awareness of the etheric body exists only within the anthroposophical world view.

In the world at large, counter-computer culture voices are rising to question the computer's impact on our bodily, soul and spiritual health. The introductory quotation, for example, is from Sven Birkerts' eloquent and perceptive book, *The Gutenberg Elegies: The Fate of Reading in an Electronic Age*. In it, he deals wisely with the difference between information and wisdom. His book achieves a process which engages. Even its reviewers become aware:

> Like a painter's slow build-up of tones, his gentle over-lappings of thoughts and themes serve to deepen his conclusions without hammering at them ... What [Sven] Birkerts does in *The Gutenberg Elegies* is to put his soul into words. *(Boston Sunday Globe)*

> His writing, which questions and muses at the leisurely pace of human speech, and which evinces both intelligence and feeling, reveals a complex individual personality, providing that kind of connectedness that a thousand e-mail messages cannot. *(San Francisco Chronicle)*

> What terrific writing ... In my more melancholy mood I hear deeper in *The Gutenberg Elegies* a most mesmeric music, and I shudder from the resonance these essays generate in my heart. *(Bloomsbury Review)*

It seems worth quoting these responses to Birkerts' book, because each in its own way manifests 'resonance.' Resonance is a quality Birkerts values. By it he means response, comprehension, engagement:

> Resonance – there is no wisdom without it ... and it cannot

flourish except in deep time ... We are destroying this deep time. Not by design perhaps, but inadvertently. Where the electronic impulse rules, and where the psyche is conditioned to work with data, the experience of deep time is impossible.[3]

This is a remarkable passage. It speaks of knowledge of the human being. Birkerts seems to be very close to saying: where Ahriman rules, and where the soul has been conditioned to work with information, experience of the etheric is impossible. He does not call it etheric; he lacks the concept. Nevertheless, 'deep time,' as characterized in *The Gutenberg Elegies,* is Birkerts' acknowledgement, albeit unconsciously, of that realm.

Another discerning observer within that surrounding, all-pervasive culture is Clifford Stoll, a computer security expert, and therefore a computer culture insider. Insider though he is, his perspective is not limited to the two dimensions of the computer screen; he is an astrophysicist and conversant with the stars, and his background and training in the astronomical dimensions of space and time give his reflections a deep, broad context. His book, *Silicon Snake Oil: Second Thoughts on the Information Highway,* is a refreshingly straightforward stripping away of the emperor's clothes. 'It's an unreal universe,' he says of cyberspace, 'a soluble tissue of nothingness.'[4] Stoll, too, honours process. He does not talk about etheric either, but he, too, recognizes the loss of life forces when he later says:

> Lotus eaters, beware. Life in the real world is far more interesting, far more important, far richer than anything you'll ever find on a computer screen.

Stoll talks about the real world, and about real time, and about real experiences in the real time of the real world. And his book is a relaxed and unpretentious but very well-informed exposé of the computer's annihilation of real experience in the real time of the real world. 'You could have been planting a tomato garden,' he goes on to tell those locked in to logging-on. 'You're viewing a world that doesn't exist.' Like Birkerts and others with similarly astute perspectives, Stoll has found resonance.[5]

But why depend on the surrounding culture for such insight? Such perspectives are welcome; but they cannot be expected to elucidate the computer's effect on the etheric realm.

In 1913 Rudolf Steiner spoke about how much more complicated than in previous eras life had become.[6] Useless to speculate on how exact his knowledge of impending technology was. But is such speculation really necessary? Don't we have enough spiritual scientific characterizations of life at the end of the century to see that the computer chip is part of a phenomenon that was foreseen, and for which anthroposophy itself is the antidote? And isn't part of that antidote being able to call the devil by his name, and being able to discern his interference with our true, human potential?

Birkerts, although presumably not a student of spiritual science, does, in fact, call the devil by his name. The final chapter of his book is called, 'Coda: The Faustian Pact.'

The devil, says Birkerts, wants our souls. 'Coda' is Birkerts' gentle but powerful assessment of the danger that has already carried us away. He struggles with the devil, page by page.

> The devil no longer moves about on cloven hooves, reeking of brimstone ... He claims to want to help us all along to a brighter, easier future, and his sales pitch is very smooth. I was, as the old song goes, almost persuaded. I saw what it could be like, our toil and misery replaced by a vivid, pleasant dream. Fingers tap keys, oceans of fact and sensation get downloaded, are dissolved through the nervous system. Bottomless wells of data are accessed and manipulated, everything flowing at circuit speed. Gone the rocks in the field, the broken hoe, the gruelling distances. 'History,' said Stephen Dedalus, 'is a nightmare from which I am trying to awaken.' This may be the awakening, but it feels curiously like the fantasies that circulate

through our sleep. From deep down in the heart I hear the voice that says, 'Refuse it.'[7]

Birkerts' struggle is deeply touching, the more so because he does not have Anthroposophia to support him. Yet, knight-like, he is true to Sophia: 'My core fear,' he writes, 'is that we are ... giving up on wisdom, the struggle for which has for millennia been central to the very idea of culture ...' (p.228).

Elsewhere he puts it like this:

> The old growth forests of philosophy have been logged and the owl of Minerva has fled ... Wisdom has nothing to do with the gathering or organizing of facts — that is basic. (p.75)

The Gutenberg Elegies abounds with profound musings which partake of the sort of insights that conscious thinking and awareness of its origins can achieve. Birkerts discerns cultural phenomena and posits a cause.

Rudolf Steiner states cause with certainty: 'No-one likes it better than Ahriman that we fail to grow wiser.'[8]

My recent reading of *The Road Ahead,* by Bill Gates, Chairman and Chief Executive Officer of Microsoft Corporation, the leading provider of software for personal computers worldwide, convinced me that Mr Gates is not so much the provider of the tool as the witless tool for the provider.

Less asleep, Stoll and Birkerts feel dis-ease. Clifford Stoll does not go so far as to implicate Mephisto in the success of the personal computer, but he does ask keenly, 'Which is the tool, the computer or the user?' Birkerts, tracking the demise of reading, writes, 'As a writer, I naturally feel uneasy.' But neither of these sensitive phenomenologists can discover the source of their malaise. It is their embattled etheric bodies, their own awareness of what Rudolf Steiner foresaw:

> Modern man ... observes the material world [he] uses his

intellect to establish the interconnections between its phenomena and believes that all its riddles are solved in this way, never realising that he is simply groping in a phantasmagoria. But this way of working coarsens and dries up his ether body, with the ultimate result that the Mephistophelian powers, like a second nature, will attach themselves to him now and in times to come.[9]

That time has come. We have lost so much vitality and imagination that we hardly notice the price of being plugged in. Mephisto/Ahriman has made it possible for humanity to invent such a neat, cheap, effective, attractive and powerful logging saw that we are dying to use it, and heedless of the price. The price far exceeds the old growth forest and the Owl of Minerva; it includes the supersensible realities that gave rise to them. We are drying up. Our life forces are being dried up. The feebler our life forces, the weaker our thinking; the weaker our thinking, the feebler our life forces. 'The world ether,' said Rudolf Steiner, 'is, in reality, the carrier of thoughts.'[10] He also said, 'Once you have really made the effort to experience thinking, you are no longer in the world you were in before, but in the etheric world.'[11] Doesn't it follow then, that once this effort is preempted, our thinking no longer partakes of the etheric world? Or that as the etheric world is sapped, thinking becomes ever more brittle. The desiccation is subtle and persistent. But not yet entirely unnoticed.

'Information, once a part of life, has swollen like a genie rising from a bottle until it threatens to become life itself.'[12] This is a clear formulation. It means: what used to be recognized as lifeless, is beginning to be considered 'life itself.' This observation is gaining coverage in the alternative media. The March/April issue of *Yoga Journal* puts it this way:

> The life force, like the sacred, exists within us. But because there are no bodies in cyberspace, no mind–body work that

> depends on the body can take place there. You can't do
> yoga asanas in cyberspace, for instance.

Incontrovertibly there are no bodies in cyberspace. Less incontrovertibly, there is no life force there. And least incontrovertibly of all, actual thinking, actual spiritual activity, cannot exist in cyberspace. Whereas we would expect to find 'life force' linked to 'body' in *Yoga Journal,* spiritual scientific study obliges us to connect 'life force' to spiritual activity, that is, thinking.

The *Yoga* article points out that, 'Spiritual and religious groups of every variety ... are seizing the virtual day.' We anthroposophists seem to fit that description. Interestingly enough, and not unrelated to the anthroposophists' cyberdilemma, the *Yoga Journal* announces its new Web sites in insets to articles questioning Internet euphoria, and pointing out its dangers. 'Can be terribly addicting,' warns *Yoga Journal;* and, underneath, a half page box with a large red heading: YOGA JOURNAL GOES ONLINE. It seems almost incomprehensible that a journal dedicated to 'a quality' of any sort should attempt to promote that quality via the Internet, especially when its announcement of such Internet promotion abuts an article that includes the assertion that experience of quality is what you cannot have in cyberspace.

Such phenomena of abstraction, of inconsistency between ideal and practice, are common. But, unlike the editors of *Yoga Journal* (and the innumerable other promoters of cyberspiritualism), spiritual scientists have a teacher who spoke plainly about the phenomenon that now surrounds us and of which we are a part.

> Man will ... chain a second being to his heels.
> Accompanied by this second being, he will feel the urge to
> think materialistic thoughts, to think *not* through his own
> being, but through the second being who is his companion.

Extraordinary words when taken in the context of the personal computer. They were spoken by Rudolf Steiner in 1914.[13] Making the personal computer a personal companion, that exactly describes what Bill Gates intended from the age of thirteen, and what he has succeeded in doing far beyond his wildest dreams.

> Back when I was a teenager, I envisioned the impact that low-cost computers could have. 'A computer on every desk and in every home,' became Microsoft's corporate mission, and we have worked to help make that possible.[14]

Bill Gates' success has made him 'the richest man in America.' Is he awake when he says 'we'?

And so it is now commonplace to 'think through the second being who is our companion,' our PC. This writer's experience may be symptomatic. For years I eschewed pen and pencil, preferring the electronic tool with its perennially clean copy. I have deliberately kept the paraphernalia limited. I still use a 386SX notebook with 1 megabyte RAM; WordPerfect 5.1. Any day now I intend to update this equipment. Primitive it may be, but it is compelling all the same, and addictive. On my sabbatical last year, I travelled a lot. Everywhere I went, my 'companion' went too. This article may be the turning point. I write these words now in humble pencil. The paragraph is raked by crossed-out words and phrases. Looking back I can see the rhythm of my toil; can see the dead ends and the tilling that preceded meaning unfolding into consciousness. No clean copy here. Not yet.

Are such traces important? Noting the evidence on this manuscript page, I see now that the answer, for me, is: yes. The involvement that came from ploughing, tilling, raking, weeding, pruning, cutting, transplanting and allowing time for composting and for watching the gradual ripening did make a difference to the fruit of my labours.[15]

More self-evident but just as unacknowledged is the physical difference between writing by hand and tapping on the keys. When you use a pen or pencil, you move your arm across the page, you see the letters traced in your own hand as you create them. You see that they are yours. It is *your* handwriting, individual enough to incriminate *you,* that flows from the tip of your pen. Imperfect perhaps, possibly inconsistent, but unique. And when your pen pauses, your eyes naturally seek the middle or far distance. You do not sublimate yourself in perfectly spaced fonts on a screen, you do not lose touch with what surrounds you. Goethe and Emerson walked to find the thoughts and words they sought. With my pencil I can negotiate thickets that seem impenetrable when I scroll through them on my screen.

But the physical flow of ink and the flow of thought it manifests are not all that is eliminated by the digital percussion on the keyboard. The flow of language itself is dashed. E-mail scrambles language into bits, acronyms, abbreviations and jargon. Even when it is not on the computer screen, language today is fragmented. Chipped. Loosed from its grammatical moorings. Severed from the 'language sense.' According to 'netiquette,'[16] it is considered rude to write in full sentences. A time-waster. Information and speed are what count, not syntax that reveals thought.

The lack of syntax and the attendant lack of thought is so common and so obvious it seems hardly worth mentioning. It is, however, a crucial phenomenon, and a perfect example is *being digital* [sic] by Nicholas Negroponte. His book is an enthusiastic affirmation of bits. Bits, he tells us, are replacing atoms. Physical objects and experience are being improved and replaced virtually. 'The change from atoms to bits is irrevocable and unstoppable.' Yes. But whereas this trend is a cause for concern to those still capable of flowing thought, it is a matter of celebration for Negroponte, whose book, although it consists of atoms, is conceived in bits. Many of its chapters are less than two pages long. They are grouped, but not related. They have clever titles. The phrases are slick, the sentences primitive, the syntax casual. There are lots and lots of info-bits. And the thoughts are definitely bits as well:

> A bit has no colour, size, or weight, and it can travel at the speed of light. It is the smallest atomic element in the DNA of information. It is a state of being. (p.14)

Surely this is a pertinent example of what Rudolf Steiner described in 1913 when he said,

> It is natural that in this era, when we are surrounded by the din of machines, human beings start thinking about everything in a materialistic way.[17]

'End-of-the-century materialism' is almost a cliché in our circles. But the phrase 'materialistic thinking' gains new force when considered in the backlit glow of our companionable machines as more and more of us rely more and more on them for the solutions to an ever-expanding variety of problems.

Machine-like thinking is spreading. The more prevalent it becomes, the less it is discerned. Like smog, it infiltrates consumingly. Clifford Stoll has noticed; and he is unequivocal: 'You subject your own thinking patterns to those of the computer.'[18] Obviously Stoll's own thinking is not yet subjugated; he resists being programmed. Though 'of the family,' he balked at Gates' gate. His common sense, his sense of life, his zest for life, his etheric forces reared up.

Others, less robust perhaps, are less fortunate. Their thinking becomes patterned. And they are unaware. Human beings who immerse themselves in computers seem to absorb some of the computer's characteristics. They are of the family, and family tics and idiosyncrasies are mindlessly accepted. *The Road Ahead* and *being digital* (as well as *Life on the Screen: Identity in the Age of the Internet* by Sherry Turkle), at least, confirm this. The computer, with its relentless consequentiality, affects its users. The 'second being who is [our] companion,' exacts a tribute; we are made to think like it.

Not surprising, then, this question: 'To what extent is human thought and creativity simply a glorified computation?'[19] This question, which depends on the computer for its existence, was raised by a journalist in the aftermath of the recent chess tournament between World Chess Champion, Gary Kasparov, and Deep Blue, a chess program.

'This was a serious opponent,' said Kasparov, who struggled, but prevailed in spite of the machine's ability to 'analyse 200 million positions per second,' a capacity called 'brute force computation.' Ironically, this brute force 'included every game Kasparov ever played, so in that sense he was playing against himself.' A matador who had programmed the bull. 'Brute force.' 'Two hundred million moves per second.' How did Kasparov win?

The computer was unable to learn during the tournament. Kasparov could, and did. In the final game, he exploited what he had learned in the previous games about the computer's weaknesses. 'At one point, for example, I changed slightly the order of a well-known opening sequence.'[20] The computer could not respond in kind.

Had Kasparov been thinking only such thoughts as can be acquired by a computer program in what is called 'knowledge capture,' he would have lost. What enabled him to win was his unmachine-like ability to learn through process, from experience. So then 'thought and creativity' are not 'simply a glorified computation.' And yet, the machine-generated question, 'to what extent is human thought and creativity simply a glorified computation?' drives the powerful research of artificial intelligence and underlies the machine-instilled illusion that computers can teach children.

If children were machines, perhaps computers could teach them. But (and it does not go without saying; it is increasingly disputed) children are not glorified computers. They are, however, prey for the machine and the 'edutainment industry' servicing the machine. It is a one-way influence. PCs are not affected by their human companions. They are not subject to the weather. They are reliable. That is one of their greatest assets. They do not have visceral reactions. They do not have viscera. The chip that stores their smarts is silicon based. They neither bloom nor fade. In them, nothing grows. Through them, thoughts are subtly relieved of elasticity. Computers, especially those hooked to the Internet, bristle with information; they have gargantuan memories, but they cannot learn. Especially from the children they are supposed to educate, they learn nothing at all. They cannot interact.

> What's most important in a classroom? A good teacher *interacting* [emphasis mine] with motivated students ... Computers promise short cuts to higher grades and painless learning. Today's edutainment software comes shrink-wrapped in the magic mantra: 'makes learning fun.' Equating learning with fun says that if you don't enjoy yourself, you're not learning. I disagree. Most learning isn't fun. Learning takes work. Discipline. Responsibility ... you have to do your homework.

This could be a Waldorf teacher, someone familiar with the concept of 'responsive tiredness,'[21] but it is Clifford Stoll, in an op-ed article in the New York Times, 19 May 1996. For Stoll, as for the Waldorf pupil, *and* the Waldorf teacher, the hard work of learning *is* the fun.

For beginning students in anthroposophical institutions, the realization that mystery wisdom cannot be memorized sometimes comes as a difficult surprise. Quite often, students entering the San Francisco Waldorf Teacher Training with successful academic backgrounds are encumbered by the expectation that their proved memorization skills and the information they acquired at university will facilitate their approach to spiritual science. Instead they encounter 'responsive tiredness' and the struggle of transformation that accompanies true learning.

Rudolf Steiner makes this comparison:

> In general we underestimate the learning ability of a child in the first days of its life. When a child learns to look into the light, more capacities are necessary than for everything one learns in the first semester at university.[22]

Learning, then, is a capacity with which the newborn child arrives, a spiritual capacity. But human learning must take place on earth. We know that the greatest lessons are taught by life itself, that we learn best by experience, hard though that school may be. The 'hard knocks of life' are proverbial. But anthroposophy scientifically informs the proverb. The concept of karma and its laws are fundamental to all of Rudolf Steiner's work. Karma *is* the path of our learning. It is in the context of karma that the aforementioned description of the infant's ability to *learn* to look into the light occurs. The achievement is of such significance that it may justify an infant death. The brief incarnation was a karmic necessity for a being who, in its previous incarnation, had been blind. Now it learns to see; 'in this case, the incarnation must be counted as part of the previous one.'[23]

Human beings learn. We learn from life, even from a brief life. Tantalizing as is the plethora of facts available via the Internet, we are in danger of mistaking the accessing and downloading for learning. The experience of learning that we take through the gate of death is just that, the *experience* of learning. As regards what we learn at the computer terminal, therefore, it depends entirely on what we do as we sit in front of a keyboard, watching digitally motivated pixels distribute themselves electronically across the screen.

Rudolf Steiner points to this:

> there is still something else to consider in respect of karma – something that ... was referred to as the process of ripening, the acquisition of a real knowledge of life. It is well to consider *how* we grow wiser. We can become wise through our faults and mistakes and this is something for which we can only be thankful. In one and the same life it is not often that we have the opportunity of applying the wisdom gained from our mistakes and it therefore remains with us as potential power for a later life. But the wisdom, the real knowledge of life that we acquire – what is it, in reality? ... It amounts to what we have acquired from experience – that and nothing more, to begin with.[24]

In the hard school of life where we learn from our faults and mistakes, one identifying feature of a karmic relationship is that it is a relationship which provides us with 'suffering and hindrances' sufficient to awaken us. That is learning. Getting flamed on the Internet is not a substitute.

In life, we use our will-motivated limbs to *walk* towards these relationships. We may be asleep to our destiny, but through our feet we may wake to it. Shackled 'by the heel' to our 'companion,' we forfeit this freedom to move into life, and accept, instead, the crude substitute of virtual movement, virtual encounter.

Concerned witnesses, such as Stoll and Birkerts, who are part of, but not party to, the culture at large, are confronting the issue of 'interactivity' by pointing out that there is nothing either 'inter' or 'active' about cyberspace encounters. Theirs is a growing chorus:

> Granted, the Internet brings people together in ways that airplanes don't. But if we want a fundamental change for the better in human relations, it will take more than the presence of a new technology to do it.[25]

> The real problem is the realization that this electronic world is, in the end, a way of encouraging separation as much as community.[26]

> Oh, the Internet is wonderful. You almost don't have to leave your house.[27]

> With crowds turning museums into pressure-cooker experiences, many people may wonder if they're not better off buying the CD-ROM and looking at Cézanne in the relative peace of their own homes. They better think again.[28]

Heartfelt though these admonitions are, the truth in them causes even greater concern when the karmically chaotic consequences of such substitute encounters become evident out of spiritual science.

The implications are great.

Just about everything anthroposophy tells us about reincarnation and karma — which, it could be argued, is its most significant contribution to modern culture — confirms the importance of human beings interacting with each other. Actually interacting with each other. So vast is Rudolf Steiner's research on this subject, that any particular quotation may obscure rather than illuminate. Nevertheless, to help focus our considerations, here are two aspects:

> Not even fifty years would suffice for you to be able to define what you can experience in five minutes as the relations of life between one human being and another. ... But if, with the help of anthroposophy, we investigate what one can really experience in five minutes but cannot describe in fifty years, we find that it is what rises up from the previous earth-life or series of earth-lives into the present life of the soul, and what is exchanged. This indefinite, indefinable element that comes upon us when we meet as adults is what shines through from earlier lives on earth into the present.[29]

> External life will become increasingly complicated — that cannot be prevented — but souls will find their way to one another through deepened inner life. ... Outer laws and institutions will make life so complicated that men may well lose their bearings altogether. But by realizing the truth of the law of karma, the knowledge will be born in the soul of what it must do in order to find, from within, its path through the world.[30]

If, then, souls are to be prevented from finding their paths through the world, they must be prevented from realizing the truth of the law of karma. Without this knowledge in their souls, without a deepened inner life, human beings will not find their way to one another. If they are prevented from finding one another, the Prince of Darkness, and not the Lord of Karma, will reign.

How to divert humanity from the 'indefinable element that

comes upon us when we meet'? How to divert souls from 'finding their way to one another through deepened inner life'? How to divert human beings from the 'knowledge of the laws of human karma that will be born in the soul'? How to divert spiritual scientists from the experience of the significance of experience and learning that spiritual science is?

Humanity is being diverted by a glittering device of irresistible allure and supernatural success.

An electronic encounter through the 'second being' is the perfect trick. It not only substitutes 'interactivity' for meetings in the earthly dimensions of space and time, it also seems to liberate us from the effort of thinking. In both instances, we are tricked into confusing Internet-bound independence from time and space with spirituality.

In a 1970 article in *The Golden Blade* John Davy, a powerful anthroposophical thinker, wrote:

> Thinking and reflective memory allow the inner life to be freed from the here and now, to roam space and time beyond the immediate situation of the body in space and its experiences of the moment.

Written before the electronic obliteration of space and time offered by the Internet, Davy's characterization of spiritual activity could be mistaken for an Internet ad. It describes, with uncanny accuracy, how the second being thinks through us when we surf the net: 'freed from the here and now, roaming through space and time.' Of course Davy was not talking about the Internet, but the applicability of his words to it shows us how neat a trick the Internet is: its least visible virtual reality is its virtual spirituality.

Likewise, interactivity in cyberspace, because it does not require people to meet in the same place at the same time, smacks of spiritual encounter. That, of course, is the purest 'phantasmagoria' – what to Birkerts, with his profound sense of time, feels 'like the fantasies that circulate through our sleep.'

In his article, Davy, in an unrelated context, deftly summarizes another fundamental aspect of karma that the Internet, with its circuits always busy, debilitates:

> The working of karma, as described by Steiner, is a rhythmic process, reflected in daily life in waking and sleeping, experiencing and forgetting, and coming to full expression in the great rhythms of incarnation into the physical world and excarnating into the spiritual world.

Birkerts, unknowingly, catches the contrast: 'Electricity is, implicitly, of the moment – *now*.'

'The computer tantalizes me with its holding power,'[31] admits Sherry Turkle, the computer sociologist, admitting at the same time that the power she is studying has her in thrall. One of her subjects goes further: 'When I MUDded with the computer I never got tired.' [MUD = *m*ulti *u*ser *d*omain, that is, an Internet 'chat room.'] In front of the artificial light of the computer screen we remain obsessively awake; yet we become bone weary, our joints ache, our eyes sting, we forget to eat, to sleep, to breathe.

Electricity is the obvious operative for technology today. Conventional physics explains some of its power. Spiritual science provides deeper insights into its inorganic force. Rudolf Steiner explains, through spiritual scientific facts seen in the context of the cosmic struggle for man's souls, *how* 'Human thinking has been altogether enwebbed by electricity.'[32]

If the chemical supersensible highs and hippie communes of the sixties did not manage to divert a whole generation from the spiritual activity of thinking and the responsibility of karmic encounter, perhaps the electronic subnatural 'companion' of the nineties and the void of cyberspace will.

And anthroposophists are not unaffected. On the contrary. The World Wide Web has every reason to strangle us:

> Opposition to anthroposophy in every domain will increase in the outside world, just because it is in the highest degree necessary for our age, and because what is the most

essential at any particular time always encounters the strongest resistance.[33]

So spoke Rudolf Steiner in a 1912 lecture cycle fittingly called, *Reincarnation and Karma: Their Significance in Modern Culture.*

Two years later, in *Technology and Art,* he pointed out in no uncertain terms, that technology was here to stay and inescapable and that trying to escape was no solution:

> It would be the worst possible mistake to say that we should resist what technology has brought into modern life, that we should protect ourselves from Ahriman by cutting ourselves off from modern life. In a certain sense this would be spiritual cowardice. The real remedy for this is not to let the forces of the modern soul weaken and cut themselves off from modern life, but to make the forces of the soul strong so that they can stand up to modern life. A courageous approach to modern life is necessitated by world karma, and that is why true spiritual science possesses the characteristic of requiring an effort of the soul, a really hard effort.[34]

So when the *Gesamtausgabe* including the Lessons of the School of Spiritual Science and their mantras appear on CD-ROM, as is all too likely, what shall we do?

What is certain is that,

> You cannot say, 'Beware of Ahriman!' for nothing can protect you from him. And if someone longs to shut himself up in a room ... where he ... is completely cut off from modern life, there are many, many ways in which Ahrimanic spirituality can get into his soul. Even though he withdraws from modern life, modern spirituality will still reach him.[35]

The Internet, then, is the cutting edge of modern Ahrimanic spirituality, and we may as well face it. Indeed, for some of us, e-mail is a professional necessity, the Internet a prime research tool. And its convenience is indisputable. Can we learn to use it without contorting karma, our own or that of others? That is what we must learn to do. *Learn* to do. With consciousness, we may mitigate the harm.

The Net is popular. Its population is now increasing at 10% per month. On the whole, it seems, the people 'in dialogue' on the Internet do not know each other. Do they get to know one another as they tap their keyboards and watch their screens? Does the sense of the ego of the other get used by cybernauts? Unlikely.

For a while we may still have the option Birkerts favours: 'Refuse it!' But, inevitably, the Internet will become the necessary communications system for Waldorf teachers, anthroposophical doctors, any of us whose professions require being 'in touch' with each other and the world.

There is, also, a more esoteric dimension to the world-wide aspect of this digital technology of international telecommunications. 'The essential characteristic of the next period of civilization is that it will not be limited to particular localities, but will be spread over the whole earth.' This is Rudolf Steiner in a lecture on *Individuality and the Group Soul,* in which he talks about how, in the future, more and more people, especially those now studying anthroposophy, will remember previous incarnations. The next sentence reads, 'Individuals will be scattered over the earth, and thus everywhere on earth, there will be a core group of people who will be crucial for the sixth epoch of civilization.'[36]

Can we, who are preparing ourselves for that future, and who are challenged by world karma to face the Ahrimanic spirituality of our time, enter cyberspace without buckling to the distortion of our Self and the future which this subnatural mockery of true communication promotes? This is the compelling question raised by Rudolf Steiner's next sentence: 'These people will recognize each other as those who in their previous incarnations strove together to develop the individual I.'

How consciously, for that matter, do we use the other electronic time and space obliterators: the telephone, answering machine and fax? The stereo, the TV? The car, the jet? Already our stereos have outpaced the relatively simple analogue technology; digital is it. 'being digital' where 'bits are states of being' is the Road Ahead.

It seems to me (and to Clifford Stoll and to Sven Birkerts) that, although the telephone and Internet are both parts of our communications technology, they cannot be compared. What is incomparable is the anonymity and the randomness of the Internet encounter. I can 'meet' anybody; I can be anybody. I can pretend to know a lot about anthroposophy. I can get involved in any controversy, fan its flames, or flame its fans. Am I responsible? To whom?

Are we preparing, at night when we sleep, to interact next day on the screen? Do our angels engage in our electronic interactivity? Or is their absence a reason for the frigidity of cyberspace?

I cannot presume to answer these questions. But having conducted many interviews with prospective students over the telephone, I can say that the attempt to cultivate attentiveness in real-time/real-space encounters helps me learn to cope with the electronic interference; I try to home in on the 'indefinable element,' in spite of the static. Can we learn to enrich our Internet encounters so that instead of 'netiquette' we exercise a capacity quite unexpected in cyberspace, namely, Logos awareness? Is that possible?

In the cyberspace environment of the Internet – an environment hostile to process, learning and deep time; electronically antibiotic; which encourages pseudo-identities, illusory meetings, illusions of loneliness overcome; where information and nonsense run wild; which dries up humanity's life forces and laces the world into a tightening, etherically depleted and depleting global web – in that environment, how will the Lord of Karma be, unless we harbour awareness of how destructive that environment is to His?

Up to the time of the Mystery of Golgotha, 'the etheric body [of human beings] became increasingly poor in wisdom.'[37] At the Turning Point of Time, this tendency was potentially reversed.

Maintaining this awareness and addressing this potential is our task.

Already in 1912, Rudolf Steiner comments on how, 'news flashes around the globe in a few hours.' This, he says, is symptomatic of a 'material civilization [which] has spread over the earth without distinction between nation and nation, race and race. ... This material culture ... will become increasingly material, and our earth body more and more deeply entangled in it.'[38] The precise technology may have been unstated, but the overall picture is prescient, and both the benefits and the danger are clear.

Spiritual science, with its conscious knowledge of cause and effect, is the medicine for the embattled supersensible environment of the earth. As the spiritual region closest to the earthly, the etheric realm promises profitable conquest for Ahriman. But the defence is extant.

In *Man As Symphony of the Creative Word,* Rudolf Steiner describes how in human evolution through the planetary stages, 'the physician preceded the patient.'[39] Now, too, the good powers of world evolution have provided us with a defence.

> The most terrible calamity would have come about in earth evolution if, in earlier ages, provisions had not been made for these experiences of Ahrimanic spirituality that world karma is bringing to modern mankind. Life always progresses like the swing of a pendulum.'[40]

Art, the legacy of Lucifer that we already have, is our defence. Our struggle to create it is our armour, for that inner struggle *is* learning and transformation. Out of that soul struggle, wisdom and growth may emerge. 'To make spiritual science your own, you must work at it in the sweat of your soul.'[41] Not electricity, but soul sweat, is the medium of our greatest learning.

E-mail may be requisite, global encounters with screen identities unavoidable, but if we work to strengthen the very forces which the Web is seeking to desiccate, we will harness the harness; gather the Internet into the context of *our* culture, rather than finding ourselves alone in a room, netted.

Ultimately, the perception that anthroposophy can illuminate for us is that the World Wide Web is a deliberate assault on the realm where we find everything that has to do with metamorphosis, process, growth, development, rhythm – time. Our thoughts, in so far as they are alive, are etherically imbued. Unlike the 'thoughts' of angels and gnomes, they require time to unfold. Time is as necessary for the development of our thoughts and the metamorphosis of a work of art as sunshine is for the growth of plants. When we allow time, and its modulation, rhythm, to be snatched from us, we allow the etheric world to be attacked.

In earlier eras it was enough to say, 'Time heals all wounds.' Today we can become conscious of the reality that forces of healing that live in time have to do with Christ's relationship to humanity since the Mystery of Golgotha, and that these forces depend on our initiative.

> The language in which we may thus speak with the Etheric Christ ... is modern anthroposophically oriented spiritual science, which in its esoteric nature represents, therefore, *the beginning of the rebirth of the teachings of the Risen Christ within humanity.*[42]

We should not wonder, therefore, that this language and its speakers are being undermined. But this too, was foreseen by Rudolf Steiner:

> It will be harder for us as Anthroposophists to make our voice heard in the world than it will be for any others. The adherents of other views of the world will have less persecution to suffer than Anthroposophists. For nothing makes men more uneasy than to describe to them the true nature of the Christ. But our conviction is based upon the results of genuine occult science and this conviction

must be sustained with all the forces of which we are capable.[43]

It will require 'all the forces of which we are capable' for anthroposophists to sustain their own forces. Eighty years ago, Rudolf Steiner predicted with compelling accuracy that:

> Very shortly, one will barely have recorded the date 2,000, there will come from America not a direct prohibition, but a kind of ... suppression of all individual thinking into purely materialistic thinking in which one does not need to work upon the soul ... and the human being is handled as if he were a machine. ... Today we have machines which add and subtract; everything is very convenient. In the future you will not get a law passed which says you must not think. No. What will happen is that things will be done which will have the effect of excluding all individual thinking ...[44]

Where shall we get the strength to abjure convenience? To discern the cloaking of our individual thinking?

> You have to develop a certain counter-weight against this tendency in world development; and anthroposophical spiritual science is this counter-weight.[45]

We shall have to *learn* how we can best sustain our forces; how least to squander them; which forces we must sacrifice, and which are sacrosanct.

References

1. Birkerts, Sven, *The Gutenberg Elegies,* Ballantine, New York 1994, p.15.
2. On 6 June 1996, a World Wide Web search for 'anthroposophy,' 'Waldorf School' or 'Rudolf Steiner,' via three major search engines (AltaVista, Yahoo and WebCrawler) yielded 2,353 posted documents and about

seventy-five Web sites. Although we cannot be certain that anthroposophists are responsible in each instance, we can deduce that we are definitely out there in cyberspace.
3. Birkerts, Sven, *op.cit.* p.15.
4. Stoll, Clifford, *Silicon Snake Oil: Second Thoughts on the Information Highway,* Doubleday, New York 1995, p.4.
5. See for example: Brook, James and Boal, Iain A., *Resisting the Virtual Life: The Culture and Politics of Information,* City Lights, San Francisco 1995; Roszak, Theodore, *The Cult of Information: a Neo-Luddite Treatise of High-Tech Artificial Intelligence and the True Art of Thinking,* University of California, Berkeley 1986; Talbott, Steve, *The Future Doesn't Compute,* O'Reilly and Associates, Cambridge, MA 1995; Tenner, Edward, *Why Things Bite Back: Technology and the Revenge of Unintended Consequences,* Alfred A. Knopf, New York 1996. Woolley, Benjamin, *Virtual Worlds: a Journey in Hype and Hyperreality,* Penguin, UK 1992.
6. Steiner, Rudolf, *Luziferisches und Ahrimanisches im Heutigen Kulturleben,* Leipzig, 12 January 1913.
7. Birkerts, *op.cit.* p.229.
8. Steiner, Rudolf, *The Great Virtues,* Zürich, 31 January 1915; in *The Golden Blade,* 1969. German text in *Das Geheimnis des Todes.*
9. Steiner, Rudolf, *The Balance in the World and Man: Lucifer and Ahriman.* Lecture of 20 November 1914, Dornach.
10. Steiner, Rudolf, *Curative Course.* Lecture of 26 June 1924.
11. Steiner, Rudolf, *Mystery Centres.* Lecture I, Dornach, 23 November 1923.
12. Edwards, Owen, 'The Infoswamp,' *Sky,* the passenger entertainment magazine of Delta Airlines, March 1996.
13. Steiner, Rudolf, *The Balance in the World and Man: Lucifer and Ahriman,* Dornach, 20 November 1914.
14. Gates, Bill, *The Road Ahead,* Viking, New York 1995, p.4.
15. To be honest, though, I have no intention of getting rid of keyboard and printer. They have their value, especially for footnotes, endnotes and editing. It is just that I now see, again, the difference writing by hand makes.
16. Negroponte, Nicholas, *being digital,* Vintage, New York 1995, p.191.
17. Steiner, Rudolf, Lecture of 12 January 1913, *"Die Welt des Geistes und ihr Hereinragen in das physische Dasein"* (GA 150). Translated by the author — no English edition traced.
18. Stoll, *op.cit.* p.45.
19. These references to the chess match from an Internet file, *Technology.* Thanks to Joseph Buller.
20. Kasparov, Gary, *Time Magazine,* 25 March 1996, p.55.
21. Steiner, Rudolf, *The Younger Generation: Educational and Spiritual Impulses for Life in the Twentieth Century,* Stuttgart, 3–15 October 1922, see Chapter 7.

22. Steiner, Rudolf, *Nature And Spirit in the Light of Spiritual Scientific Knowledge,* Stockholm, 8 June 1913. Published in *Anthroposophical News Sheet,* no.3, 1935.
23. Ibid.
24. Steiner, Rudolf, *The Mission of Christian Rosenkreutz: its Character and Purpose.* Lecture of 8 February 1912, Vienna, 'The True Attitude to Karma.'
25. Galletta, Dennis F., in *The Press Democrat,* 19 February 1996.
26. Goldberger, Paul, in *The New York Times,* 5 October 1995.
27. Quoted in an article by Wendy Lapides in *The Pacific Sun,* 6–12 March 1996.
28. Perl, Jed, 'Is It Real or Is It Megabytes?' *The New York Times,* 1 June 1996.
29. Steiner, Rudolf, *The Younger Generation,* p.146.
30. Steiner, Rudolf, *Reincarnation and Karma. Their Significance for Modern Culture.* Lecture of 21 February 1912, Stuttgart.
31. Turkle, Sherry, *Life on the Screen: Identity in the Age of the Internet,* Simon and Schuster, New York 1995, p.30.
32. Steiner, Rudolf, quoted by Ernst Lehrs in *Spiritual Science, Electricity and Michael Faraday,* Rudolf Steiner Press, London 1975, p.17.
33. Steiner, Rudolf, *Reincarnation and Karma. Their Significance for Modern Culture.* Lecture of 5 March 1912, Berlin.
34. Steiner, Rudolf, *Art as Seen in the Light of Mystery Wisdom.* Lecture of 28 December 1914, Dornach, 'Technology and Art.' p.16.
35. Ibid., p.18.
36. Steiner, Rudolf, *The Universal Human: The Evolution of Humanity.* Lecture of 4 December 1909, Munich, 'Individuality and the Group-Soul.'
37. Steiner, Rudolf, *The Gospel of St John in Relation to the Other Three Gospels.* Lecture of 5 July 1909, Kassel.
38. Steiner, Rudolf, 'The Death of a God and its Fruits in Humanity,' Düsseldorf, 5 May 1912. In *The Festivals and Their Meaning,* Rudolf Steiner Press, London 1981.
39. Steiner, Rudolf, *Man As Symphony of the Creative Word,* Chapter 10, Dornach, 9 November 1923.
40. Steiner, Rudolf, 'Technology and Art.' See reference 48.
41. Ibid.
42. Prokofieff, Sergei O., *The Cycles of the Year as a Path of Initiation,* Temple Lodge Press, London 1991, p.157.
43. Steiner, Rudolf, *The Mission of Christian Rosenkreutz.* Lecture of 27 January 1912, Kassel.
44. Steiner, Rudolf, "Things of Present and Past," lecture of 4 April 1916, Dornach. Manuscript translation of *"Zeichen, Griff und Wort"* in *Gegenwärtiges und Vergangenes im Menschengeiste* (GA 167).
45. Ibid.

Shakespeare and world destiny

Richard Ramsbotham

In attempting to approach the being of William Shakespeare we are faced with very particular difficulties for, as with no other writer, with the exception perhaps of Homer, we know next to nothing about Shakespeare's actual biography. As if this were not enough, we are then faced with the further difficulty that this very lack of information has led many to posit that Shakespeare's works were actually written by someone else, and that William Shakespeare was merely a mask for that other person, or for a whole group of people. (The most notable claims for the 'true' author of Shakespeare have been made for Francis Bacon, Lord Bacon of Verulam, or for Christopher Marlowe, or for the Earl of Oxford, or for a whole circle of people, a Rosicrucian brotherhood, including, for example, the Elizabethan magus and mathematician, Dr John Dee.)

There is undoubtedly a mystery in this fact of Shakespeare's having been 'everyone,' in his work, where we feel the whole of humanity walks before us, and 'no-one' in his own life, to the point of even seeming to have no biography.

This has often been written about, for example by Owen Barfield, who describes the 'uneasy feeling' one may have, that Shakespeare:

> does not mean anything. He has nothing to say. His characters know what they mean and can utter it in the most beautiful language. They know also what they want, have individuality. Not so the author. He is, indeed, 'not

one but all mankind's epitome.' He has no existence apart from the characters.[1]

It is a mystery, furthermore, that makes it extraordinarily difficult to approach the individuality of Shakespeare, as one might any other great artist or figure from history, with a view to exploring their karma and destiny. Rudolf Steiner, who, up to the present time, has alone been able to speak publicly about the previous incarnations of a wide range of significant individuals, from differing spheres of life, nowhere, to my knowledge, spoke about the karmic past of Shakespeare, although he did so with regard to one of Shakespeare's characters, Hamlet.[2] This is entirely in accord with the mystery of Shakespeare, of which we have been speaking.

The time may come, however, when one nevertheless feels the need to get closer to the individuality of William Shakespeare. It is out of such a need that the present article has arisen. The article may be seen as an attempt to work along the lines Athys Floride suggests, in the second part of his book *Human Encounters and Karma,* the part entitled 'Encountering A Poet Through His Work.'[3] It does not come from any perception of, or speculation about, former incarnations of William Shakespeare. It consists, rather, of the initial steps I have been able to make, in the attempt to approach William Shakespeare, as an individuality, at all.

Now, although Rudolf Steiner did not speak specifically of Shakespeare's karmic background, he did speak in detail about Shakespeare several times. These pieces have seldom attracted much attention, as they are far from sensational in character, even seeming, at times, almost to be going out of their way to state the obvious. And yet, if we can read them rightly, they turn out to provide a germinal starting point.

Wherever people have questioned the identity of Shakespeare, they have always agreed that there was an actor, called William Shakespeare, who grew up and died in Stratford-upon-Avon, and who must have acted in many of the plays that bear the name of

Shakespeare. They say, however, that this actor, William Shakespeare, did not write the plays, but was merely a mask for the person, or persons, who did. This is almost always the assumption, furthermore, that a mere actor could not possibly have possessed what was necessary to write the plays of Shakespeare.

If we were to condense into a single sentence much of what Rudolf Steiner says about Shakespeare we might put it thus: the most important thing of all about the plays of Shakespeare is *precisely* that they were written by an actor.

Let us now explore this more fully in order to see the approach it offers us, both to Shakespeare and his works.

In 1898 Rudolf Steiner wrote an essay entitled, *Another Secret of Shakespeare's Works*,[4] in which he sets himself the goal of discovering what Shakespeare's 'world view' may be said to be. Having described Goethe's 'world view,' for example, and that of other writers, he says that Shakespeare cannot, in any comparable sense, be described as having a world view. If he has a world view, says Steiner, it is one we should call 'the dramatic world view,' by which he means that Shakespeare's approach to every single situation is to seek purely for what is 'dramatic' in that situation.

This point is developed further and further in everything Steiner later said about Shakespeare. We must understand what he means by it. It is perhaps easier if we make an analogy with another art, painting. Despite its sounding almost impossible to the non-painter, one recognizes that the truest painters do not start with an idea that then determines colour and form, but create *out of the colours themselves*. The colours themselves, in their development and interrelationships, become the determining factors. In a similar way, says Steiner, Shakespeare did not create out of any ideas he had about his characters, or in order to express any point of view, or world view, but created *out of the dramatic medium itself*. What is truly dramatic in a situation or character — what will bring them to life most fully on the stage — is the determining factor in Shakespeare's plays.

In a lecture given in 1902 about Shakespeare, Steiner speaks again about this phenomenon:

> It is useless to ask what Shakespeare's own standpoint may have been on certain questions ... Whether Shakespeare believed in ghosts and witches, whether he was a churchgoer or freethinker, is not the essential point at all; he simply faced the problem: how should a ghost or a witch appear on the scene so as to produce a strong effect upon the audience?[5]

He then adds:

> The fact that this effect is undiminished today, proves that Shakespeare was able to solve this problem.(!)

This essentially dramatic quality of Shakespeare's plays, Steiner tells us, is to be found, in the same way, in no other playwright, and is the reason for his unceasing popularity worldwide. Furthermore, it was a quality which, by definition, could only be achieved by someone with the most intimate and practical knowledge of the theatre and, primarily, of acting itself. It is no accident, therefore, that one can choose to overlook, but rather a necessity, discoverable from the plays themselves, that Shakespeare was an actor:

> Shakespeare's own works bear witness that he is their author. His plays reveal that they were written by a man who had a thorough knowledge of the theatre and the deepest understanding for theatrical effects ... In the whole literature of the world there are no plays which are so completely conceived from the standpoint of the actor. This is a clear proof that Shakespeare, the *actor,* has the merit of having written these plays.[6]

Only twenty years later, in 1922, in Stratford-upon-Avon, on Shakespeare's birthday, 23 April, does Rudolf Steiner reveal the full spiritual consequences of Shakespeare's way of creating.

Shakespeare's characters, reiterates Steiner, are not mere imitations of life, or the result of intellectual ideas, but are created specifically for the stage. The chief task Shakespeare set himself was, therefore, *to create.* To create, in the world of the theatre, *beings who live,* who are fully alive. And because Shakespeare was so successful in this, the remarkable fact is that, if, through spiritual vision, one can transfer one's experience of Shakespeare's characters into the spiritual worlds, the characters continue to live there. So fully alive are they that they continue to live through all worlds, performing actions there quite different from those they perform in the plays. And this is not at all the case with lesser dramatists.

> Shakespeare is a theatre-realist, he creates for the stage ...
> He knew that it is not possible to produce characters on the stage, which are imitated from life ... Shakespeare is not an imitator of life. Shakespeare is a creative spirit who works with the material that lies before him. In this way he created his living characters, that enable us to look into the astral plane, into Devachan and into the whole spiritual world. There, these characters do something which is different from what they do on the physical plane. Yet they are alive, they *do* something.[8]
>
> A Man's life of any worth is a continual allegory – and very few eyes can see the Mystery of his life – a life, like the scriptures, figurative – Shakespeare led a life of Allegory; his works are the comments on it. (John Keats)[9]

Despite all that we have said, we will, of course, if we wish to come closer to William Shakespeare, have to look at his plays to see what they can reveal about him. The fact that Shakespeare did not set out to express any 'message,' or point of view, but worked primarily as a 'creative spirit,' does not mean that we cannot learn anything from his plays, only that it will be very important *how* we approach them.

Because Shakespeare's characters and plays *live,* they undergo metamorphosis, and this we are able to observe. Rudolf Steiner remarks:

> people always try to look for the logic in Shakespeare's plays. However, they are guided not by logic but by the pictorial element.[10]

This is particularly so in that drama speaks in *stage-pictures*. We must learn to see the pictures that each play speaks in, and then see how these metamorphose from play to play. By this means we may gradually start to read the Mystery of Shakespeare's life that is hidden in his plays, as Keats so beautifully describes.

We will return, later, to the significance of Rudolf Steiner's remarks about the essentially *dramatic* character of Shakespeare's works. For now, however, let us plunge into the pictures of his plays and see how they develop from play to play. We will see how all of the plays together form a great whole — D. H. Lawrence called it 'the great novel of Shakespeare' — with the situation and events of one play metamorphosing into those of the next, and with the characters, as it were, reincarnating from play to play. Once we have immersed ourselves in this, we will come back to see what this can tell us of Shakespeare himself.

In *Hamlet,* if we approach the play as picture, or pictures, what do we find? The pictures are many, and are of such a nature that we can immediately understand how their life and being could never be restricted to the play alone. For many of us they form a part of our own inner world — the death of Ophelia, for example, in the 'glassy stream,' or the ghost of Hamlet's father appearing on the battlements, in the cold winter's night, in Denmark. Of all of them, however, there is one which we might justly think of as the central, archetypal image of *Hamlet.* Hamlet himself, in the graveyard, while Ophelia's grave is being dug, holding a skull in front of him — Yorick, the jester's skull — and meditating on it. It is a moment out of time, in a sense, yet it is not a static image. It is part of a moving, living imagination. Shortly afterwards Hamlet 'leaps into the grave.'

This helps us to sense the development that takes place during *Hamlet*. In this central image of the play, Hamlet comes to terms with death — meets it face to face. It is through this that Hamlet is transformed. We remember Hamlet's fear of death, earlier in the play:

> To die, to sleep;
> To sleep: perchance to dream: ay, there's the rub;
> For in that sleep of death what dreams may come
> When we have shuffled off this mortal coil,
> Must give us pause.

How totally different he is, after the graveyard scene! With what freedom from fear, and freedom to act, Hamlet enters the duel in which he is, in fact, to die. Horatio suggests that if Hamlet feels uneasy they should delay the action. Hamlet will not hear of it, knowing that death will come when it will:

> If it be now, 'tis not to come; if it be not to come, it will be now; if it be not now, yet it will come: the readiness is all. Since no man has aught of what he leaves, what is't to leave betimes? Let be.

Hamlet, we may say, is obliged to come to terms with a new relationship between man and the world, unknown in medieval times, where man has, as it were, *fallen out of* the order of things:

> The time is out of joint; O cursed spite
> That ever I was born to set it right!

He succeeds in this, as we saw in his all-important facing of death, in the form of the skull. The fact of its being a skull is significant, furthermore, in that Hamlet's battle is fought out in consciousness, in the sphere of the head, primarily. The place where the play begins is telling: 'on the high platform under the frosty stars.'[11]

In *King Lear,* written five years after *Hamlet,* the sphere where the action takes place has shifted, as A.C. Harwood points out. The same battle as in *Hamlet* has, in a sense, to be fought out, no longer merely in the consciousness, however, but now in the deepest levels of man's being, in the tumultuous, unconscious realm of the will. The victory, if it can be won, will be far more profound in its consequences but, for the same reason, will cost infinitely greater suffering to achieve.

Lear's story is, put simply, that of his being stripped, layer after layer, of everything that had previously given his life meaning, of everything that had previously given him his identity. It can therefore be nothing other than a journey towards madness. Step by agonizing step, the layers are peeled away – kingdom, daughters, retinue, walls, clothes, senses – until nothing is left.

At the beginning of the play, Cordelia had answered 'nothing' when ordered by Lear to speak of the quantity of her love for him. Lear, in fury, had banished her – banishing, at the same time, his own heart, for Cordelia, as Ted Hughes points out, is also 'Coeur de Lear.' Now, at the end of the play, Lear, himself, in his nakedness, has also been brought to nothing:

> Pray do not mock me:
> I am a very foolish fond old man
> ...
> And, to deal plainly,
> I fear I am not in my perfect mind.

It is, at this moment, that the miracle can begin. Cordelia's 'nothing' was, of course, only a seeming nothing; once it is reached, it proves to be merely a gateway to an infinitely richer sphere of being, beyond. And so precisely now, when Lear has lost himself, he finds himself, anew, and can be reunited with Cordelia:

> Do not laugh at me;
> For, as I am a man, I think this lady

To be my child Cordelia.
Cordelia: 'And so I am, I am.'

And then after all this, Cordelia is taken away from him, and murdered. Lear must walk in holding her dead body in his arms. The pictures in *King Lear,* as in *Hamlet,* are many, and are lasting, but this is the truly shattering one. In some periods people have found it too terrible to behold, and have changed the ending so that Cordelia does not die. But, if we would travel the path of Lear, we must, with him, somehow suffer it through. ('Suffering through,' or 'patience' – stemming from 'pati,' meaning 'to suffer' – is perhaps *the* crucial virtue in all of Shakespeare, and certainly in *King Lear.*[12])

Lear's pain is too great for words, and so he enters howling:

Howl, howl, howl, howl! O! You are men of stones:
Had I your tongues and eyes, I'd use them so
That heaven's vaults should crack. She's gone forever.

For a brief moment, Lear believes that she lives, and knows that if this be true it would make all his former agonies worthwhile:

if it be so,
It is a chance which does redeem all sorrows
That ever I have felt.

But it is not so. Cordelia is 'dead as earth,' as Lear is forced to recognize:

Thou'lt come no more,
Never, never, never, never, never!

After this, Lear himself can hold on to life no longer but, in his last moments, looking at Cordelia's mouth, where he had hoped to see signs of breathing, he suddenly sees something that no-one else sees:

> Do you see this. Look on her, look, her lips,
> Look there, look there!

and he dies.

In *The Winter's Tale* we are again faced with a stormy, Lear-like male, in Leontes. Again, he perpetrates the most terrible crimes on the female; far worse ones, in fact, than King Lear did. Believing, without any basis whatsoever, that his wife, Hermione, has been unfaithful to him, he throws her in prison, and tries her, with the clear intention of condemning her to death:

> thou
> Shalt feel our justice, in whose easiest passage
> Look for no less than death.

Meanwhile, in prison, the queen has given birth to a daughter – their second child – and, certain that he is not the father, Leontes orders Antigonus to have it burned alive:

> If thou refuse
> The bastard brains with these my proper hands
> Shall I dash out. Go, take it to the fire;

Leontes is only just persuaded out of this, and commands that Antigonus take it instead to some foreign land, and abandon it to its fate:

> bear it
> To some remote and desert place quite out
> Of our dominions; and ... there ... leave it
> Without more mercy, to its own protection,
> And favour of the climate.

No figure in Shakespeare does greater wrong than Leontes. And yet, unlike *King Lear,* the journey of *The Winter's Tale* is one that leads, eventually, to a 'happy ending.' In *King Lear,* the whole play is necessary for Lear to undergo the trials that enable him to be reunited with Cordelia. In a purely earthly sense, it is too late.

No sooner is Lear reunited with her than Cordelia is murdered. Lear walks in holding her dead body and, shortly thereafter, dies himself. In *The Winter's Tale,* Leontes, like Lear, is to be reunited with the daughter he banished but, although Leontes' actions were *far* crueller than Lear's, the reunion, in *The Winter's Tale,* is miraculous and lasting, and the very opposite of tragic.

Leontes' wife, Hermione, is tried for adultery — on sentence of death. A message from the oracle at Delphi arrives, proclaiming that: 'Hermione is chaste' and Leontes 'a jealous tyrant; his innocent babe truly begotten.' Leontes demands that the trial continue, declaring that the oracle lies. At that moment news comes that the son of Leontes and Hermione — their first child — has died. Hermione falls unconscious and is taken out, and, suddenly, the veils fall from Leontes' eyes. He sees what terrible wrongs he has done, but too late, for Paulina returns to announce to him the greatest of all his wrongs — the queen, Hermione, is dead. Leontes vows unending penitence, and exits, saying: 'Come and lead me / Unto these sorrows.'

But we are only in the middle of the play, not at the end of it. Events will now weave in a most remarkable way, so that Shakespearean tragedy will be overturned, will end in healing and redemption, and not in woe. The message from the oracle at Delphi had added that Leontes would never have any heir: 'if that which is lost be not found!' This refers, on one level, of course, to his baby daughter, Perdita, who has been left to die, in the open, in a foreign land. On another level, it refers to all that, on an inner level, man has lost, that he has to re-find.[13]

Perdita, then, with all that she represents, must somehow be refound by Leontes, and the rest of the play consists of the journey that must be trodden to make this possible.

At the end of Act Three, we see Antigonus abandoning Perdita in Bohemia, as the dead queen, Hermione, had instructed him to do, in a dream. The baby is found there by a shepherd, and Act Four then begins sixteen years later.

Bohemia is ruled over by Polixenes, the former friend of

Leontes, whom Leontes had sought to have killed, believing him guilty of adultery with his wife. Polixenes has a young son, Florizel, the heir to the throne of Bohemia. Perdita, meanwhile, has grown into a young woman of almost goddess-like beauty: 'no shepherdess, but Flora / Peering in April's front.' Florizel has chanced upon the shepherd's cottage, where Perdita lives, the two of them have fallen boundlessly in love, and wish to be married immediately.

Polixenes discovers this and, furious that his son should woo a shepherd's daughter, threatens Perdita with death and Florizel with disinheritance if they even speak of their love again. The two young lovers, who will not be parted, are advised by the wise Camillo to set sail for Sicily, and find Leontes, who, eager to atone for the wrongs he had done in the past, will be sure to help them, and rejoice in their wedding celebrations.

And so Act Five sees Perdita, her identity unknown, even to herself, returned to Sicily and, standing in front of Leontes, beseeching his help, with Florizel. That which Leontes has lost has been found again. He does not know it yet, although his words reveal it: 'Welcome hither, / As is the spring to the earth.'

Shortly afterwards, however, events so unravel that everything is made known. Polixenes has also come to Sicily, as have the two shepherds who brought Perdita up, and who are threatened with death by Polixenes. Everyone meets together – Leontes, Polixenes, Perdita, Florizel, Paulina and the shepherds. The shepherds, to save their lives, tell of how they found Perdita, and show the letters and other things that had been left with her.

It is a reunion far more total than that between Lear and Cordelia, and is one that beggars all description. It is 'a sight, which was to be seen, cannot be spoken of.' It is therefore not acted out on the stage, but is narrated to the audience, by people who witnessed it.

There is another reason, though, why it is not acted out. In *King Lear* the reunion between Lear and Cordelia was, in a sense, the high point of the play. It could not be maintained, and was followed by the searing image of Lear carrying Cordelia's dead body. In *The Winter's Tale,* the reunion of Leontes and Perdita *is* maintained and therefore leads up to the highest resolution that must form the chief image at the end of the play. We learn, together with the whole assembly, that Paulina has, in her keeping, a statue of the late Queen, Hermione, and they all go to 'a chapel in Paulina's house' to see it. Much is said of how this statue represents the highest achievement possible to art.

Paulina unveils it, and Leontes, speechless at first, remarks:

> I am asham'd: does not the stone rebuke me
> For being more stone than it?

Shortly afterwards, almost out of his senses, but happy to be so, he says, gazing on the statue:

> methinks,
> There is an air come from her: what fine chisel
> Could ever yet cut breath? Let no man mock me,
> For I will kiss her.

We remember Lear, with Cordelia's body, howling:

> O! you are men of stones

then holding a mirror to Cordelia's face, and saying:

> If that her breath will mist or stain the stone,
> Why, then she lives.

Should this be so, he said, it

> does redeem all sorrows
> that ever I have felt.

It was not so, in *King Lear,* but now, in *The Winter's Tale,* that redemption is happening. The stone is melting human hearts and then the stone, itself, is being seen to breathe. Death is being turned to life.

Paulina steps forward and says to everyone present: 'It is

requir'd / You do awake your faith.' Then, after telling those to leave 'that think it is unlawful business / I am about,' she announces that she can, indeed, make the statue walk, and take Leontes by the hand. Leontes beseeches her to do so, at which Paulina addresses the statue:

> 'Tis time; descend; be stone no more; approach;
> Strike all that look upon with marvel. Come;
> I'll fill your grave up: stir; nay, come away;
> Bequeath to death your numbness, for from him
> Dear life redeems you.

'Hermione comes down,' Leontes is presented to her, and they embrace. Only one thing more is now necessary in order that Hermione may not only be brought back to life, but may also speak. Paulina asks Perdita to kneel before her mother, then says to Hermione:

> Turn, good lady;
> Our Perdita is found.

Hermione speaks, first to the gods, then to Perdita, and the play ends on the highest possible level of rejoicing, redemption and resolution.

The pictures in *The Tempest,* Shakespeare's last play, work differently, more visibly, than in the other plays. It, nonetheless, picks up clearly from where *The Winter's Tale* left off, and thus represents the furthest stage of development and metamorphosis of Shakespeare's plays.

In *King Lear* the whole play was needed for Lear and Cordelia to be reunited and this could not last, on earth. In *The Winter's Tale,* at the end of the play, not only have Leontes and Perdita been successfully reunited but, in the coming back to life of Hermione, we have seen what might be called magical powers restored to man. In *The Tempest,* this is where we begin. Prospero (the Leontes/Lear character) and Miranda (the Perdita/Cordelia character) are together, from the start, and Prospero is a magus on a grand scale. What, one might ask, remains to be achieved? In the answer to this lies the riddle of the difference of *The Tempest* from the other plays. To explore the details of this, however, goes beyond the scope of this article.

Let us now turn our attention again to what Rudolf Steiner said about the essentially 'dramatic' nature of Shakespeare's work and see, in conjunction with the picture-journey we have made through the plays, what this can reveal about the being of William Shakespeare.

What does it mean to construct plays not out of any philosophy, or world view but, first and foremost, out of what is experienced as dramatic? It means, of course, that, as in all creative endeavour, it is not possible to work out of any previously held conceptions. But does it not also mean that something must *live* in the dramatic — that behind, or within, drama there must be a being who will speak through the work, if, like Shakespeare's, it is created purely out of the dramatic itself? Rudolf Steiner suggests that this is so, by stating: Something transcending ordinary human life lives in drama. Shakespeare entered deeply into this.'[14]

Who is this Being, then, who stands behind true drama? Emil Bock addresses this question in his book *The Three Years*.[15] He begins by saying that 'properly understood, the Gospels contain archetypal drama,' and then makes the surprising statement that 'the drama of the Gospels and the drama of ancient Greece are intimately related.' He explains this by saying that what the ancient Greek drama did was to make public 'both consciously and unconsciously, part of the ancient Mysteries.' This connects it to the Mystery of Golgotha, which 'represented the entire and final public revelation of the principle of the Mysteries.' Since that time, says Bock, 'the archetypal drama has been in the very midst of humanity.' The significance of this for drama itself and its rebirth is that, from that time on, it: 'can and must be fertilized by the central archetypal drama of humanity which took place on Golgotha.'

SHAKESPEARE AND WORLD DESTINY

The work of William Shakespeare is unarguably the greatest single contribution to the rebirth of drama in Christian times. Is it possible to say, however, that his work has been 'fertilized by the central archetypal drama ... which took place on Golgotha'? Let us look once again at the picture-development through Shakespeare's plays, and we will see that it certainly is possible for us to say this, and in the most remarkable of ways.

The key is given to us in *King Lear*. We saw the central image there to be Lear carrying Cordelia's dead body in his arms. With no effort at all this image transposes itself into that of the Pieta – of Mary carrying Christ's body, or of Joseph of Arimathea, taking Christ's body from the Cross.

The central image of *Hamlet* we saw as that of Hamlet, in the graveyard, holding a skull and meditating on it, before he 'leaps into the grave.' A little more poetic licence, admittedly, and we see *Hamlet* as Shakespeare's 'Place of the Skull.' It is Good Friday, the stage of the Death on the Cross, Crucifixion, which precedes the image depicted in *King Lear*.

The central image of *The Winter's Tale* is, without question, the miraculous and heart-rending one of the statue, Hermione, descending and returning to life. The significance of this may evade us until we realize that what we are in the presence of is *the stone moving*. *The Winter's Tale* represents, in terms of the unfolding of the 'archetypal drama ... which took place on Golgotha,' Resurrection, or Easter Sunday.

In *The Tempest* the images do not happen, on stage, in the same way as in the other plays. Nonetheless people have rightly seen as central to the whole play Prospero's speech, which closes the grand spiritual celebrations of the true union of Ferdinand and Miranda:

> be cheerful sir:
> Our revels now are ended. These our actors,
> As I foretold you, were all spirits and
> Are melted into air, into thin air:

> And like the baseless fabric of this vision,
> The cloud-capp'd towers, the gorgeous palaces,
> The solemn temples, the great globe itself,
> Yea, all which it inherit, shall dissolve,
> And like this insubstantial pageant faded,
> Leave not a rack behind. We are such stuff
> As dreams are made on, and our little life
> Is rounded with a sleep.

Is the content and mood of this and, indeed, of much of *The Tempest,* anything other than that of Ascension?

We can even go so far, I think, as to say that the Epilogue to *The Tempest,* where Prospero tells us that everything now depends on how others receive what he has done, points towards the Mystery of Whitsun.

Death on Golgotha, the taking down from the Cross, the Entombment, Resurrection, Ascension – step by step, in his own way, Shakespeare treads the path of Christian Initiation.[16] This is what our researches reveal.

There is a further point, connected to this. Sergei Prokoffief, in *The Cycle of the Seasons and the Seven Liberal Arts,* describes how the different arts each relate to a specific Festival. Thus Whitsun relates to the seventh art, the social art, and Ascension to eurythmy. Easter relates to 'the art of the word.' It is:

> the art of the word that can approach most closely to the
> mysteries of Golgotha. The works of this art form stand
> like great milestones in the history of humanity and,
> through them, human beings can acquire an understanding
> of the full significance of the Mystery of Golgotha.[17]

I hope that this article has shown that this last sentence is wholly applicable to the works of William Shakespeare.

This may well lead us to ask: What is the specific relationship of the being of William Shakespeare to the Easter Mystery, the Mystery of Golgotha? It is this Mystery which we have seen to underlie, in the most intimate and individual of ways, the development of his plays. The circumstances of Shakespeare's life also ally him deeply to this time: he was born and died on the same day, 23 April, St George's Day, which falls between Easter and Ascension.

William Shakespeare, in the details of his life and his work, shows himself to be united, in the profoundest way imaginable, with the true Source of drama.

References

1. Barfield, Owen, 'The Form of Hamlet,' in *Romanticism Comes of Age*, Wesleyan University Press 1986.
2. Steiner, Rudolf, *Lectures on The Gospel of St Mark*, Lecture 1. Anthroposophic Press, New York 1986.
3. Floride, Athys, *Human Encounters and Karma*, Anthroposophic Press 1990.
4. Printed in *The Anthroposophical Quarterly*, Christmas, 1928.
5. From: 'Notes of a Lecture by Rudolf Steiner at the Workman's School in Berlin, 1902.' *Anthroposophical News Sheet*, Vol.13, 9–10, Jan. 1935.
6. Ibid.
7. Shakespeare and the New Ideals, included in *Waldorf Education and Anthroposophy*, 1, Anthroposophic Press 1995.
8. 'Rudolf Steiner's Report on his Lecture Tour in Holland and England in 1922.' *Anthroposophic News Sheet*, 24 February 1935.
9. Letter to George and Georgiana Keats, February 14–May 3, 1819.
10. *Waldorf Education and Anthroposophy*, 1, Anthroposophic Press 1995, p.216.
11. Harwood, A.C., *Shakespeare's Prophetic Mind*, Rudolf Steiner Press, London 1977, p.41.
12. Lear, in Act II, as one by one his former 'needs' are denied him, prays: 'for true need, – / You heavens, give me that patience, patience I need!' In Act III, refusing to answer the Fool's jibes, he says: 'No, I will be the pattern of all patience; / I will say nothing.' There are many other remarkable references to patience throughout the plays. Pericles, for example, says to Marina: 'thou dost look / Like Patience gazing on kings' graves, and smiling / Extremity out of act.' *Pericles,* Act V, Scene 1.
13. See the wonderful linking of *The Winter's Tale* with the myth of Persephone

and Demeter, in *Shakespeare's Flowering of the Spirit,* by Margaret Bennell, Lanthorn Press 1971.
14. *Waldorf Education and Anthroposophy,* 1, Anthroposophic Press 1995, p.229.
15. Bock, Emil, *The Three Years,* Floris Books 1980, p.181.
16. See Bock, Emil, *op.cit.* pp.172–74; also Steiner, Rudolf, *The Theosophy of the Rosicrucian,* Rudolf Steiner Press, London 1966.
17. Prokoffief, Sergei O., *The Cycle of the Seasons and the Seven Liberal Arts,* Temple Lodge Press, 1995, pp.22–23.

Karma and the mystery dramas

John Gee

Rudolf Steiner began his very last lecture series – the Speech and Drama course (1924) – by emphasising that anthroposophical endeavour does not arise out of the 'urge to plan reforms' or 'put out some great "idea" into the world' but rather arises out of the attempts to meet the 'demands of karma.' Karma, he stresses, is the guiding principle in all anthroposophical endeavour. The challenge it would seem then is to awaken to the opportunities that our karma provides us with in order to bring to realization on the earth impulses for spiritual renewal. We need, in other words, to begin to awaken to the reality of reincarnation and karma.

It is not surprising that Rudolf Steiner was to emphasise this point in the introduction to a lecture series devoted to the renewal of dramatic art. For could one not say that the idea of reincarnation and karma is the very archetype of all dramatic art? Does it not seek in essence to present on the stage the drama of the reincarnating individual? Shakespeare, for instance, hinted at this when Jacques in *As you like it* refers to the world as a stage where we have our 'exits' and 'entrances' and where we 'play our many parts.' We meet the archetype in the image of the 'actor' and the 'stage.' Wherever drama approaches 'mystery' drama, the archetype comes to the fore. But this archetype was not fully revealed until Steiner himself wrote his four Mystery Dramas (1910–13). For the very first time in the history of drama the reincarnating individual is presented on the stage in his full reality. Reincarnation and karma is the very lifeblood of these dramas.

We are thus presented with scenes that take us back in time beyond the characters' present earthly life. We are given glimpses of dramatic moments in their past lives on earth – the consequences of which are affecting their lives at present. These images from the distant past help them to understand the problems and difficulties that they are facing now in their present relationships with one another. We are presented with a new perspective of human evolution, as we see the characters evolving from life to life, gradually awakening to their eternal humanity through their ever-deepening relationships to one another.

Here, then, in the Mystery Dramas of Rudolf Steiner we have one way in which we can begin to awaken to the reality of reincarnation and karma – we can take into ourselves the example of the characters as they struggle to awaken to this reality in their lives.

Words of the initiate character Benedictus in the first drama *The Portal of Initiation* sound as the leitmotif that echoes on through all four dramas:

> Here in this circle a knot forms out of the threads that
> karma spins in world becoming. (Scene 3)

In this karmic 'knot of destiny' lies the 'seed' of the karmic task of this particular group of people. They have the possibility of creating something new if they can gradually take hold of their karmic ties from the past and transform the threads of destiny that have bound them together in a 'knot.' Benedictus has the task of constantly drawing their attention to this possibility. He helps those who are ripe for it to awaken to their karmic tasks with respect to one another. But it is they themselves, the individual characters, who must ultimately unravel the karmic knot. Only free deeds of love performed in the name of Christ can fully redeem past karma, it is revealed. Few of the characters have the inner strength and courage to do this fully. They are continually pitted against the forces of evil in their soul life, that would draw them away from doing this – often with tragic consequences for the whole group. But every little step taken in this direction by one or the other helps in the gradual realization of their karmic task – which, in the case of this particular group of people, is to lay the foundations for a modern mystery centre.

Through conscious acts of sacrifice certain individuals can take it upon themselves to share in the karma of another person or, as in the case of Benedictus, even the karma of the whole group. But each is called upon in his own way to awaken to his particular karmic task within the group. One is reminded of the apocalyptic words of the old Man with the Lamp in Goethe's fairy-tale *The Beautiful Lily and the Green Snake* (1795) – a work that was the major source of inspiration for the Mystery Dramas:

> The old Man looked up to the stars, and then began to speak: 'We are assembled at the propitious hour; let each perform his task, let each do his duty; and a universal happiness will swallow up our individual sorrows, as a universal grief consumes individual joys.' At these words arises a wondrous hubbub: for all the persons in the party spoke aloud, each for himself, declaring what they had to do.

It was very much in the spirit of these last words that a group of us, who eventually founded the English Mystery Drama Group, began our work with the Mystery Dramas nine years ago. We had long felt the need to begin a dramatic work together. Various attempts had been made but nothing really came of these. It was only when a certain question was put to some of us that we really found the impetus to begin the work – the question whether performances of the Mystery Dramas would help draw the wider anthroposophical movement together in an open celebration of the very heart of anthroposophy. We wondered whether the Mystery Dramas could be a source of inspiration for community building. The question acted as a kind of catalyst drawing us together. It worked as the 'seed' around which we could crystallize our work. We experienced it as the 'star' that was to guide us through many a storm on our voyage into uncharted waters. It seemed like 'a star of destiny.'

Presumably the 'time was at hand' for the dramas to be more widely performed in English. The work grew rapidly over the following years with performances of the dramas to ever-increasing and divergent audiences in many parts of Europe and North America. Performances of the dramas seemed to meet a need in the hearts of many people. We often heard members of the audience say that experiencing the dramas gave them a feeling of hope.

Working on Rudolf Steiner's Mystery Dramas one cannot really avoid being drawn into the question of karma and how it works in life. Indeed, it is a great privilege to have the opportunity to work intensively on dramas that in both their form and content are focused on the question of karma itself. Looking back over the past nine years, it seems to me that one could say that both the achievements and failures of the work are the result of our attempts to face the question of karma. The work seems to have arisen out of the constant struggle on the part of many people to awaken to a karmic task together – the struggle to somehow take hold of karma and try to raise it towards free deed. This feels like an undercurrent that has gone through the work. Sometimes in the actual act of performance one could feel that we had perhaps broken through to something new.

In all that we have gone through together I think it would be true to say that it is the Mystery Dramas themselves that have been our constant guide. We have, as it were, had to *live* the Mystery Dramas both in our own personal lives and in our lives together as a group. We have had to face the same kind of trials and temptations as the characters in the drama as we have tried to work together. We have had, from time to time, to take on the role of Benedictus for one another, in our attempt to awaken to 'the knot of destiny' that seemed to have bound us together to do the work. It has been a challenge not to lose sight of the 'star' that had originally brought us together. We would often feel, as we worked on a particular drama, how the serial dynamic of the karmic relations between the characters in the drama seemed to find its echo in the serial dynamics of the group itself. Our own mystery drama seemed in many ways to be echoed in the Mystery Dramas themselves. We could thus find a constant reference point for what we were going through in trying to recreate the dramas, in the inner gesture and dynamics of the dramas themselves. Thus, working on the dramas one developed a heightened awareness of the dynamic of karmic relations working between us. It was as if one was meeting an archetype in the dramas.

We were constantly faced with new challenges, as we worked our way through all four dramas. I think we experienced the greatest challenges in working on the last one, *The Soul's Awakening*. In this drama the characters themselves are continually challenged to try to overcome the things that separate them from one another, to try to find one another anew, to build a 'bridge' towards each other in order that they can work fruitfully together for the benefit of mankind. Particularly deep levels of karma are at work in their meetings with one another. We witness, in the Temple scene, the events that have triggered off the karmic dynamic between them – a failed initiation ritual in Ancient Egyptian times. Here in this event lies the 'seed' of their karmic task – to create a new form of temple – a 'human' temple of the spirit. They can hardly be said to have achieved this by the end of the day. In many ways they appear to have failed. The powers of darkness do all that they can to lead them astray. We feel the tragedy of our own times. But through their experiences and ordeals they find new powers of hope that will lead them on into the future.

It was always an enormous challenge to work on this Temple scene and in many ways uncomfortable. It was the scene that called up the greatest degree of conflict in the rehearsal period. One could feel that one had to overcome oneself in order to work on as if one was on the edge of something in the dynamic of the group's own karmic relations. It was the scene that in many ways resisted one and required the greatest degree of presence of mind in performance. It was the scene in which one felt perhaps most naked as a group. One could not but ask oneself the question — what events in *our* karmic past have triggered off the dynamics of karmic relations between *us*? Why are we standing here now performing Mystery Dramas together?!

Awakening to the reality of reincarnation and karma is perhaps one of the greatest challenges in our time — something that concerns the whole of humanity. Through such an awakening we will be able to find the moral forces that will be needed if we are to lay the foundations for human community in the future. Working with Rudolf Steiner's Mystery Dramas can be a help towards this awakening. Through working with these dramas I believe one can begin to develop an organ for recognizing the working of karma in the dynamic of our relationships. One becomes more intensely aware of this dimension of our human existence. And although the dramas present unique karmic situations and relationships, one wonders whether there is, all the same, an archetype going through all four dramas — in the dynamic and gesture of these relationships — that applies to all 'temple building' between human beings who are consciously striving to work together out of the impulses of a modern mystery wisdom. And, as we awaken to this in our own lives together, maybe we will be writing new dramas for the theatre of the next century!

Notes on the contributors

Dr Virginia Sease is a member of the Executive Council of the Anthroposophical Society and leader of the Section for the Arts of Eurythmy, Speech and Music.

Nick Thomas is Chair of the Anthroposophical Society in Great Britain, and is actively engaged in research in projective geometry applied to physics.

Nothart Rohlfs has worked as a gardener, translator and author, spent five years in Järna and is now active in independent adult education and research.

Hans Peter van Manen is a historian, teacher, author and lecturer.

Hartwig Schiller has been a Waldorf teacher and is now a member of the faculty of the Waldorf Teacher Training Institute in Stuttgart.

Dorit Winter is director of the Rudolf Steiner College Extension Course Teacher Training Programme in San Francisco.

Richard Ramsbotham taught English literature at Warsaw University and is now a student at the Speech School, Peredur Centre for the Arts, where he also teaches literature.

John Gee is a graduate of the Speech School, Peredur, and has taken part in all four Portal Productions of the Mystery Plays.